To Rome With Love

A Study In The Book of Romans, Part One
By Anne Nicholson

Copyright © 2021 Anne Nicholson

All rights reserved. No part of this book may be reproduced by any means, graphic, electronic, or mechanical, including photocopying, recording, taping or by and information storage retrieval system without the written permission of the author except in the case of brief quotations embodied in critical articles and reviews.

Scripture taken from the New King James Version®, Copyright © 1982 by Thomas Nelson.
Used by permission. All rights reserved.

THE HOLY BIBLE, NEW INTERNATIONAL VERSION®, NIV® Copyright © 1973, 1978, 1984, 2011 by Biblica, Inc. ®
Used by permission. All rights reserved worldwide.

Scripture taken from the Amplified Bible, Copyright © 1954, 1958, 1962, 1964, 1965, 1987 by The Lockman Foundation.
Used with permission.

Books may be ordered through booksellers or by contacting:

Open Heavens Publishing
1369 Burke Lane
Auburn, AL 36830
www.annenicholsonauthor.com
openheavenspublishing@gmail.com
334.329.4142

Because of the dynamic nature of the Internet, any web addresses or links contained in this book may be changed since publication and may no longer be valid. The views expressed in this work are solely those of the author and do not necessarily reflect the views of the publisher, and the publisher hereby disclaims any responsibility for them.

Any people depicted in stock imagery provided by Getty Images are models,
and such images are being used for illustrative purposes only.
Certain stock imagery © Getty Images.

ISBN: 978-1-9537-4206-3
Library of Congress Control Number: 2021905974
Print information available on the last page.
Open Heavens Publishing rev. date: June 15, 2021

List of Weekly Lessons and Scriptures

Part I: The Redeemed And What We Believe
Romans Chapters 1 – 11

A. Righteousness Of God vs. Unrighteousness Of Humanity

#1	Romans 1:1-17	Paul's Greeting To The Romans
#2	Romans 1:18-32	God's Wrath Against Humanity - The Gentiles
#3	Romans 2:1-3:8	God's Righteous Judgment - The Jews And The Law
#4	Romans 3:9-20	The Depravity of Mankind

B. Forgiveness of Sin Through Christ: Righteousness Imputed - Justification

#5	Romans 3:21- 4	Through Christ Abraham Is Justified By Faith
#6	Romans 5	Destiny: Death Through Adam & Life Through Christ

C. Freedom from Sin's Grasp: Righteousness Imparted - Sanctification

#7	Romans 6:1-14	Dead To Sin And Alive In Christ
#8	Romans 6:15-23	Slaves To Righteousness
#9	Romans 7:1-13	A Portrait Of Marriage
#10	Romans 7:14-25	The Struggle With Sin

Introduction

Greetings!

Welcome to part one of a two-part study in the book of Romans. Together, we are embarking on a remarkable journey to embrace the love, liberty, and grace of this most beloved Epistle. Theologians have called it the most important letter ever written. That should make us all sit up and take notice!

Let me say that again; it has been called the most important letter ever written. Consider this. Since hieroglyphics, millions, possibly billions of love letters have been written, but this is it. Romans is #1, even today. Why? Because its timeless message is so powerful that it still eclipses the great works of literary giants like Shakespeare, Emerson, and Tolstoy.

Although Paul penned Romans through the inspiration of the Holy Spirit, its author is God. Scripture confirms that God is love, and that's His overarching message in Romans. Theologians agree if it were all you had of scripture, you would have enough. Enough to come to an understanding of who God is, and in light of that who you are, and enlightened awareness of God's love-filled plan to save sinners.

By examining Romans' text, you will discover that God and His salvation plan are eternal. His purpose has existed from eternity past, it's rooted in love, and that will never change. At this very moment, God's love for you is absolute. It's whole! Consequently, you can't do anything more, different, or better to cause God to love you more than He already does and already has. Paul knew all about God's love, grace, and forgiveness. The benefits, naturally and spiritually, are found in every verse. No place in scripture is divine love more clearly defined than in Romans.

The deep things of God are there, too. Every element of God's profound theological works are navigated, explored, and explained - it's the doctrinal book of the Bible. Beyond that, Romans unites believers, defines boundaries, and outlines God's plan for Israel, the original recipients of divine grace. Romans settles questions like, "What will happen to the Jews?"

Finally, Paul ends the letter by outlining right Christian living. Paul is straightforward; he makes it simple and concise. He concludes the Romans' letter by imploring us to come into agreement with God and finish strong. That's a finish that brings honor and glory to the name Jesus and above all else - it benefits the gospel.

Make It A Personal Journey. I want to encourage you to make this study a personal journey. Approach each lesson and biblical text prayerfully, as if Paul's letter was written just to you. Although the message does not omit one element of fundamental doctrine, the overarching theme is love. Through Romans, God's love for humanity, the pinnacle of His creation, His image-bearers and purveyors of love, hope, and truth on the earth comes to light. Historically, Romans has been identified as the believer's Declaration of Independence. It's also our biblical Constitution and Bill of Rights. In short, its 16 chapters consisting of 9,447 words rightly teach, affirm, and define what we believe and why we believe it. It's God's plan – not man's. In light of that knowledge, Romans teaches us how all believers should behave.

The esteemed Epistle has been melting the hearts of men since Phoebe delivered it from Corinth to the church of Rome in 57 AD. Although she is not singled out for this service in scripture, many biblical scholars believe that she was its courier. If so, this would make her the only woman to deliver an original biblical text to its recipients. Be encouraged and take note of this. Throughout history, God has called, anointed, and equipped women to be His vessels and servants – agents of His Holy Word.

If Paul were with us today, and you asked him to name his most significant work, he would no doubt confess the book of Romans. Through the centuries, its inspired words have birthed every great awakening of the church. Noted theologians, men like Irenaeus, Augustine, Martin Luther, Karl Barth, George Muller, John and Charles Wesley, David Brainerd, and countless others have been so moved and inspired by its text that each was ushered into a heightened revelation of God's grace and perfect plan to save sinners. When its life-changing words take root in a heart, everything else pales in comparison. We see vividly that salvation, from start to finish, is a holy and sacred work of God with divine meaning and divine purpose. Salvation has always been a work of the Trinity.

It's All About God. Reading and studying Romans brings God front and center because the revelation of Christ shapes every chapter and verse. It gives us the profound opportunity to know the God who loves us, calls us, and saves us - personally. Moreover, it gives us purpose to pause and reflect on His righteousness and our created need for Him. Ladies, we need God, and Jesus will meet us in every verse. So, anticipate Him! Through its pages, we will truly delight to worship, adore, and praise our great God and King – Jesus. *To Rome with Love* is titled as such because the book of Romans drips of love. His lavish love for you! Romans' words will pierce even the hardest hearts and break off fallacies and wrong doctrine because it mercifully aligns us with God. Then we can love Him like never before, with pure hearts of worship. To know God and His plan for humanity is the reason we study Romans. Ladies, knowing God is the reason we embark on this journey today!

Love and Blessings,
Anne

Note: Unless otherwise indicated, all scripture is taken from the NKJV. Scripture taken from the New King James Version®. Copyright © 1982 by Thomas Nelson. Used by permission. All rights reserved.

About The Study Guide

The Romans study is designed to promote reflection, prayer, confession, liberation, and response. Each week, your higher purpose is to understand God's Word and come into agreement with it. The study adopts a five-day format, which is outlined below.

Day One - **Read.** Day One introduces the week's passages through a series of questions designed to grow us in knowledge, understanding, right living, and the will and purposes of God. Every week, the overarching question is: "What does God say?"

Day Two - **Research**. You will Identify, investigate, and define ***keywords*** and ***key phrases*** in the week's text which provide elements of foundational doctrine. Romans is full of words and passages that we must know, understand, and embrace as children of God. We don't want to miss out on their dominant meaning or application. Words such as justification, sanctification, glorification, etc., will be examined. Additionally, difficulties in the text will be pinpointed, studied, and recommended for further group discussion.

Day Three - **Receive.** In light of our primary text, you are called to come into agreement with God. Our Lord desires that you open your heart to receive His truth, remembering that your mind is renewed by God's living word as it washes over you and is empowered by the Holy Spirit. (See Romans 12:2.) As you come into agreement with God, your soul will find spiritual refreshing as it is fed, nourished, and satisfied.

Day Four - **Reflect**. While examining the text, you will ask and answer, "What is God speaking to me, personally?" "Do I have an accurate understanding of God's Word in these passages?" "Is change needed in any area of my life?" You will be invited to take an honest look deep within as you examine your heart and motives in light of God's Word.

Day Five - **Respond.** You are invited to walk in the liberty and victory of transformation. You are ready to embrace the world around you. That always begins in a humble setting among those who know you best and love you anyway - your family and real friends. With a liberated and joyful heart, you will be challenged to bring your behavior and attitude in line with your confession of faith. Fully embracing God's truth, you have the unprecedented honor and privilege of imitating

Christ. Rejoice, today you respond by moving forward in the strength of the Holy Spirit to righteous living and loving like Jesus!

A Word Of Encouragement. No one ever studied God's Word and remained the same, particularly the epistle to the Romans. This beloved, life-changing revelation of Christ is challenging, liberating, and inspirational. It is my opinion that if you marinated only in Romans for your remaining days, you could finish strong, transformed, and completely satisfied.

Each week, I highlight passages that have spoken expressly to my heart. Look for them! They are called: ♥ **Heart-Check For Today**. Each lesson will also include a memory verse. Please commit it to memory and prayer. From time to time, you will be invited to journal or write a prayer that reveals what God's Spirit is speaking to you from the selected passages. I hope you enjoy the journey. You're in for an amazing spiritual transformation.

Lesson 1: Paul's Greeting To The Romans
Romans 1:1-17

Day One: **Read**. Romans 1:1-17.

Memory Verse: "For I am not ashamed of the gospel of Christ, for it is the power of God to salvation for everyone who believes, for the Jew first and also for the Greek. For in it the righteousness of God is revealed from faith to faith; as it is written, 'The just shall live by faith' " (Romans 1:16-17).

Background: Throughout our study, we will pause to look at Paul, the author of Romans. He was once the Pharisee of Pharisees and a confessed chief of sinners. He worked tirelessly to destroy the early church seeking out believers and persecuting them was his mission. He participated in the stoning of the first recorded martyr in scripture, Stephen. (See Acts 7.) But God had a plan and apprehended Paul on the road to Damascus, and Paul was forever changed! That blinding and radical conversion reshaped Paul's heart. His zeal for destruction and persecution was replaced by keen spiritual insight and passion for the Lord Jesus. Paul's focus changed; he was a new man with a new mission. That mission was the advancement of the Kingdom of God and winning souls to fill it. And what a call it was! He would stay singularly focused all the remaining days of his life. Under the Holy Spirit's inspiration, he authored 13 books of the New Testament and possibly Hebrews. Paul determined "not to know anything among you except Jesus Christ and Him crucified" (1 Corinthians 2:2). Like Jesus, he placed no confidence in men, and he remained focused and true to his pledge throughout his days.

A Roman Jew from Tarsus, Paul had always desired to travel to Rome. Sometimes things don't happen the way we think, not even for Paul. However, his understanding that God is in control and is "working all things together of good" (See Romans 8:28) provided comfort and purposed Paul to wait upon the Lord. Over time, it became apparent that the Church at Rome needed sound doctrine. Paul got to work in preparation for his upcoming visit. To settle doctrinal disputes and correct fallacies, Paul got to work. In agreement with Paul, one modern-day theologian said it like this, "The only real cure for bad doctrine is a biblical doctrine." So, Paul sat down, filled with God's spirit, and wrote the most profound love letter ever written. In keeping with God's plan, these living words have been liberating hearts and converting sinners for more than 2000 years. Isn't God amazing? If Paul had gone to Rome, there would have been no need for him to pen this most beloved Epistle, a doctrinal work of genius. In a nutshell, that more than describes the book of Romans. Paul's inspired words assure us of our need for salvation and then provide us with the best account of our spiritual transformation in the whole of scripture. It is not surprising that Romans is considered the most theological book ever written.

Paul eventually made the journey to Rome, shackled in chains. There he was imprisoned until the time of his beheading. Both he and Peter were ultimately martyred in Rome.

1. Read Romans 1:1. Paul identified himself in three ways in this passage. List them below.

2. Paul was ready to lead. Read the words of Jesus in Matthew 20:26-28. How does Jesus define a true leader?

3. a. Using a dictionary, define *humility*.

b. Review Romans 1:1. Based on your definition of humility, would you say that Paul has assumed a position of humility or greatness?

4. Paul was called by God. If you're saved, you're called too! Has God expanded your call into a position of leadership? If so, please share a brief testimony of your call.

5. Provide a biblical definition of *servant* below. Who was Paul serving?

6. Read Romans 1:2. Notice the phrase, "the gospel he promised…". Indeed, the gospel had been promised. Record an old testament prophecy that points to the promised gospel.

7. Read Romans 1:3-4. Record everything that these verses record about Jesus Christ.

v. 3

v. 4

8. Read Romans 1:5-6. Record everything that these verses record about you as the redeemed of God.

v. 5

v. 6

9. Read Romans 1:7. Who does Paul specifically address, and what does he extend to them?

10. Read Romans 1:8-15 and answer the following questions.

　　Who does Paul thank? v. 8

　　Who is his witness, and whom does he serve? v. 9

　　What specific *way* did Paul wish to travel? v. 10

What was Paul hoping to accomplish? v. 11

What was the mutual bond they shared? v. 12

Lesson 1: Paul's Greeting To The Romans
Romans 1:1-17

Day Two: **Research**

Prayerfully read Romans 1:1-17.

I. Using a dictionary, bible dictionary, or concordance, define the following *keywords*.

a. *bondservant* v. 1:1

b. *apostle* v. 1:1

c. *gospel* vv. 1:1, 9, 16

d. *grace* vv. 1:5, 7

e. *saints* v. 7

f. *faith* vv. 1:5, 8, 12, 17

II. Read the following **key phrases**:

separated to the gospel v. 1 - literally, separated to the "good news." The term means "*to separate oneself, to be cut off.*" The passive tense of the verb in Greek implies that the separation is being imposed on the subject by God. In other words, this is God's work! That would confirm the apostolic call of Paul. The definition from *The Greek-English Lexicon of the NT* states "*to set aside a person for a particular task or function 'to appoint, to set apart for.'*"

Separate/separated (*aphorizō*) the verb appears ten times in nine NT verses. For another example of divine separation, read Acts 13:2 and record the words of the Holy Spirit.

Acts 13:2 -

born of the seed of David according to the flesh v. 3 - Jesus had a human birth; therefore, He had a body of flesh and bones just like you. Unlike you, He was entirely God and fully man. As prophesied, He lived a life of ***flesh*** and blood born from the ***seed*** of a woman. (See Genesis 3:15.) Romans 1:3 testifies of His humanity, while Romans 1:4 announces His deity. The resurrection validates and confirms His claim to deity. Jesus fulfilled his self-proclaimed prophecies when He rose from the dead.

spirit of holiness v. 4 - Only Christ was perfect, holy, and sinless. Only He could live a sinless life and die in our place. We will look at this closely in a few weeks. In our text, the ***spirit of holiness*** refers to Christ's inner spirit. He lived His life in complete and perfect holiness, in harmony with God. Record Luke 2:40 below to see another example of Jesus' spirit of holiness. The Greek word used in both passages is "pneuma." Luke 2:40 is the first scriptural reference of Jesus' "inner spirit" following His human birth. Record Luke 2:40 below.

Luke 2:40

obedience to the faith v. 5 - True saving faith always produces obedience and submission to Jesus Christ. We trust Him, we love Him, and we obey Him. Jesus said it plainly in John 14:15. Prayerfully record John 14:15 below.

John 14:15

Beloved of God v. 7 - literally *loved by God*. The Greek-English Lexicon of the NT states, "*pertaining to one who or that which is loved—'object of one's affection, one who is loved, beloved, dear.'*" This is how God feels about you! Read Matthew 3:17 and 12:18. Note: In Matthew 12:18, God not only loves Jesus but something extra as well. Record the additional information from Matthew 12:18 below.

Matthew 12:18

fruit among you v. 13 - Paul was looking to win other Gentiles to the Lord. Once converted, teaching and preaching the good news of the salvation of Christ became his sole mission and purpose in life. Remember, Paul was burdened for the Gentiles because that was God's plan! Paul was called and chosen to minister to the Gentiles! (See Acts 9:15.) We know it was not his practice to minister on another man's foundation. We will study this in Romans 10. Although burdened for all Gentiles, it's possible that the Romans uniquely captivated Paul's heart. Paul was a Roman citizen who had never been to Rome! Theologians agree that Paul's Roman citizenship came through his father's bloodline because Judaism always passes from mother to child. To return to Rome and win Roman Gentiles for Christ was always on Paul's heart.

♥ <u>Heart-Check For Today</u>.

What's on your heart? Where is your Rome? Is there some place that you are dying to share the good news? What about within your family? Paul had a kingdom focus, do you? Read Acts 1:8. It's the call of the global church. That means it's your call, too, because if you're saved, you're called! Record Acts 1:8 below.

Record Acts 1:8

preach the gospel v. 15 - literally, proclaim or herald the good news of the salvation of Christ. The message was from God and about God's plan. The gospel is the *"good news"* that God will forgive your sins, deliver you from the grip and power of sin, and give you eternal hope - which is everlasting life. The best news is that we can't earn it. Salvation is God's free gift to all who receive it, repent, and believe. Read and record Romans 10:12-13 below.

Romans 10:12-13

ashamed of the gospel v. 16 - Focusing on the word "ashamed," *The Greek English Lexicon of the NT* states, *"to experience or feel shame or disgrace because of some particular event or activity—'to be ashamed of.' "* Paul was not humiliated, disgraced, embarrassed of the good news. He was humbled and honored to preach the gospel of the salvation of Christ. Paul recognized that he was an apostle simply by the grace of God. Read the words of Jesus from Mark 8:38. What is the warning from this passage?

Mark 8:38

Lesson 1: Paul's Greeting To The Romans
Romans 1:1-17

Day Three: **Receive**

Memory Verse: "For I am not ashamed of the gospel of Christ, for it is the power of God to salvation for everyone who believes, for the Jew first and also for the Greek. For in it the righteousness of God is revealed from faith to faith; as it is written, 'The just shall live by faith'" (Romans 1:16-17).

Not only is Romans 1:16-17 our memory verse, but it is the thesis of the entire book of Romans. Paul will teach from this foundation throughout the book. These passages are so significant. It has been argued that along with John 3:16, these are the most critical passages in the whole of scripture. These words transformed Martin Luther's life, which led to the great Reformation of the church. While studying and teaching through the Epistle of Romans, Luther had a spiritual awakening. He received a divine revelation concerning salvation which comes by faith alone. The results? He was forever transformed. His transformation has impacted us because the Reformation put God's Word into the hands of ordinary men - hungry sinners – and all God's people - including you. As we journey through Romans, may you be enlightened as well!

1. Some weeks, we will record our memory verse. For reinforcement of these powerful words, record Romans 1:16-17 below. As you write the words, ask God's Spirit to bring you into all knowledge and understanding of their meaning. Receive God's Holy Word.

2. Romans 1:16-17 highlight nine significant themes in the book of Romans. Review the thesis verse and complete these tasks. 1). Locate and **circle** each word or phrase in the verses which highlight the corresponding theme. 2). Locate and **underline** the "means" by which righteousness is revealed.

gospel
power of God
salvation
faith
life of faith/live by faith
Jew/Gentile
righteousness from God
revelation/revealed
righteousness by faith

3. Read Romans 1:16-17 again. Paul was not ashamed of the gospel. Think about the first phrase, "I am not ashamed of the gospel." Can you think of a time when you have been ashamed of the gospel?

4. ♥ <u>**Heart-Check For Today.**</u>

Paul was not ashamed of the gospel. He was never intimidated by hostile crowds or fear of rejection. He had the good news for all who would believe. He knew the gospel was a stumbling block for the Jews and foolishness to the Gentiles, but he also knew it was the power of God unto salvation! Paul could preach it because it is the power of God. It's powerful! It saves! Are you actively sharing the gospel and trusting God for the results? If not, what's holding you back?

5. Looking at the second phrase, "…because it is the power of God for salvation for everyone who believes." Scripture always confirms itself. Do these inspired words bring other similar scripture to mind? Please record a confirming verse(s) below.

6. Read Romans 1:16. Whose work is salvation? Who was to receive it first? Who was to receive it afterward?

7. The basic meaning of salvation is *deliverance or rescue*. Having received that free gift of salvation, we are delivered from many things. Read each scripture to identify "*how, or through what means, or source*" we are delivered from many things. Record your findings below.

　a. from being lost: Matthew 18:11

　b. from the wrath of God: Read Romans 5:9

c. from evil self-indulgences: Read Galatians 5:19-26

d. from the penalty of our sins: Romans 6:23

e. from eternal separation from God: John 5:24

8. Read Romans 1:17. Whose righteousness is revealed in the gospel? How is it revealed?

9. Review Romans 1:17. How is righteousness received? What does that mean?

10. Look at the phrase, "The just shall live by faith." In Greek, the word **shall** is in the indicative mood. In this case, that tells us that the verb's action, *living by faith*, is being presented as "real – authentic - a fact – accomplished - a done deal." Greek's indicative mood consistently portrays something *as actual as opposed to possible or contingent on intention.* It is ours; it's done. With that in mind, when we come to faith, we live by faith. What does it mean to you personally to live by faith?

Lesson 1: Paul's Greeting To The Romans
Romans 1:1-17

Day Four: **Reflect**.

Prayerfully Review Romans 1:1-17.

1. The text of Romans quotes OT scripture more than 50 times. We find an example in the last phrase of verse 17, "The just shall live by faith." Yesterday, we affirmed through Greek grammar that the redeemed of God **live by faith**. We find this four times in scripture. In addition to our memory verse, similar words are found in the NT in Galatians 3:11 and Hebrews 10:38. Similar words appear in the OT as well. Bible scholars agree that Paul was quoting the OT prophet, Habakkuk, in Romans 1:17. (See Habakkuk 2:4.) From its OT usage, we see that this is not a new concept. Even in the OT, **righteousness could only be obtained on the basis of faith.**

Record Galatians 3:11

What additional information is revealed in Hebrews 10:38? Record it below.

Record Habakkuk 2:4

2. James had much to say about faith. Record your favorite verse below, which speaks to believers living out their faith.

3. It is important to note that faith is not the end but the beginning. What does faith produce? Cite a passage to support your answer.

4. You were invited to define faith on day two. God has defined it for us in His Word. Read and record Hebrews 11:1 below.

5. Biblical faith produces a life lived in harmony with the will and purposes of God. It glorifies Him! That faith, from beginning to end, is living and active. It always produces the good fruit of action. Over time, as faith grows and develops, it nurtures our character and gives us a loving, submitted attitude toward every command and requirement of God. We look and live like Christ! Does this describe your faith? Are you looking more and more like Christ? If not, what is holding you back? You are invited to share.

6. Apart from the power of the Holy Spirit, we can't live in harmony with the will and purposes of God. We must abide in Christ and continually ask to be filled with the Holy Spirit, praying to bear good spiritual fruit by His grace and for His glory. Read and record the fruit of the spirit from Galatians 5:22-23.

7. ♥ **<u>Heart-Check For Today</u>**.

Look at the list from Galatians 5:22-23 and then ask yourself, "How am I doing in the area of loving, patience, and self-control, etc.?" Be honest because this is how we grow. Perhaps you are feeling unloving, or lack patience, etc. Take a few minutes to pray through these verses. If you feel unfruitful, ask the Lord to bear great fruit in this area of your life. Ask someone to unite with you in prayer about it. Then walk in believing faith that it is accomplished. If you'd like, you are invited to share. Your insights might be beneficial to others. Be discreet.

8. Scripture assures us that troubles will come into our lives. Believers are not exempt from disappointment, heartache, sickness, or even death. Remember, we are saved in this world, not from this world. Nevertheless, **the just shall live by faith**! Has your faith ever been challenged? Perhaps it is being challenged now. We will all endure trials and hardships; life is not easy. Ladies, it's not heaven until heaven. You are invited to share a testimony of a time that your faith was challenged. How did you respond? How did the Lord redeem it all?

9. Complete the following passage from James 1:2-8 concerning biblical faith.

James 1:2-8 v. 2 My brethren, count it all _____ when you fall into various trials, 3 knowing that the testing of your faith produces _____. 4 But let patience have *its* _____ _____, that you may be _____ and _____, lacking _____. 5 If any of you lacks _____, let him ask of _____, who gives to all _____ and without _____, and it will be given to him. 6 But let him ask in _____, with no _____, for he who doubts is like a _____ - of the sea driven and _____ by the wind. 7 For let not that man suppose that he will _____ anything from the _____; 8 he is a _____ man, unstable in all his ways.

10. We will define biblical faith as follows: Biblical faith is confident obedience to God's word despite the circumstances consequences. This describes Abraham's faith. Does it describe yours?

Lesson 1: Paul's Greeting To The Romans
Romans 1:1-17

Day Five: **Respond**. Prayerfully Read Romans 1:1-17

Memory Verse: "For I am not ashamed of the gospel of Christ, for it is the power of God to salvation for everyone who believes, for the Jew first and also for the Greek. For in it the righteousness of God is revealed from faith to faith; as it is written, 'The just shall live by faith' " (Romans 1:16-17).

Before you begin your prayerful response to God's word, let's pause to think about this week's scriptural journey. Paul has definitely laid a powerful foundation to launch our study in the book of Romans. He has succinctly brought the gospel of the salvation of God front and center.

To sum it all up, faith has always been the means of grace by which God saves us. It has always been based on faith alone – in Christ alone. That is such good news because if you had to work to earn it, you would never know for certain that you had done enough. It is all God. It always has been. He knew we could never accomplish what was required to satisfy the wrath of a Holy God. Who among us is good in and of ourselves? Paul has assured us, "There is none righteous, no, not one" (Romans 3:10).

As we conclude our study, let's look briefly at two crucial phrases in Romans 1:17. They are too important to overlook. They are "from faith to faith" and "the just shall live by faith."

First, Paul assures us that faith activates the revelation of the righteousness of God from *faith to faith*. When you believe and come to faith, instantly, that excellent righteousness of God is imputed (credited, assigned, attributed) to you. How amazing! You are declared righteous and holy, and God has done it all. You didn't earn it. You can't buy it. You believed, and it was your gift because God extended you the means of grace to believe. That faith saved you, and even now, His keeping faith is at work to sustain your belief. In other words, that same faith that saved you by the grace of God will keep you until the end. Although it will grow, mature, and deepen on the journey, it will not be finished in this life. You will not be complete until you stand before your Maker. Yes, from faith to faith, you are kept just as God has promised. He will see you through!

Next, by assuring that *"the just shall live by faith,"* Paul affirms that through saving faith, you have life and will live forever! Thanks to a merciful God and His perfect plan, you are alive, presently, and you will live in eternity in the presence of Christ because you have faith in Christ alone.

So, what of faith? Is that it? Or does it have a life of its own? Let's examine some biblical elements of authentic faith, saving faith that keeps us. Hint: Saving faith is not dead!

Saving Faith Is Obedient And Enduring

1. **Faith obeys.** Saving faith is obedient to God's word and delights to do the will of God. Abraham obeyed. Read Hebrews 11:8. By faith, what was Abraham called to do?

2. **Faith worships.** Abel worshiped. Read Hebrews 11:4. Abel offered something by faith. What did he offer, and what did he obtain? Note: His offering was more excellent and the first act of worship recorded in human history. (See Genesis 4:3-8.)

3. **Faith walks with God.** Enoch did. Read Hebrews 11:5. What did Enoch not see?

4. Faith works to accomplish the will of God. Noah did. Read Hebrews 11:7. How was Noah moved, what did he accomplish, and what did his action condemn?

5. Faith believes God - always! Abraham, the "Father of faith," did. Despite the circumstances or consequences, Abraham believed God completely. That means that Abraham believed what God said (His Word) and believed in His ability to perform it. Did you catch it? That's the standard of faith. According to God's word, Abraham's faith sets the standard for all who believe. Read Genesis 15:6. What did God do when Abraham believed?

An overview of Hebrews 11 further reminds us that "by faith," others prevailed. Some, having conceived out of barrenness and overpowered death. Additionally, saving faith emboldened the saints of old to trust in a God they couldn't see or touch for everything, even their futures. They abandoned earthly treasure and instead looked with anticipation to their heavenly reward. By faith, they conquered kingdoms and performed righteousness acts. They obtained the promise and shut the mouths of roaring lions. Some endured the furnace while others put the enemy to flight. By faith, they received miracles from God and dared to face great danger with poise and dignity. That's saving faith, and it endures to the end. It stands the test of time.

Since the beginning of time, faith has empowered saints to overcome death, endure extreme afflictions, and resist temptation. Faith has survived, endured, and conquered every unspeakable manner of hardship. Why? **Saving faith lays hold of the gospel of the salvation of God!** And if that weren't enough, when faith ignites in belief, you are given His spirit, which is Christ in you, the hope of glory. Until the end, through it all, this saving faith remains. He will never leave you or forsake you! Saving faith will keep you until God calls you home.

To sum it up, authentic faith (saving faith) always produces or manifests actions and attributes which imitate Christ. God's redeemed look like Jesus. They walk like Him, they talk like Him, serve like Him, give and forgive like Him, and once found, they embrace their kingdom purpose like Jesus! Paul surely did, and all the saints of Hebrews 11, although not perfect, demonstrated faithfulness that mattered to God. How do we know? God says so - they made the Book!

<u>Now is your time to respond</u>. Pray through these questions and settle all matters of doubt, insecurity, or uncertainty. Thank the Lord Jesus for all that He has done on your behalf. The Lord Jesus is waiting for you! May you be mightily blessed as you enter into His presence!

Is your faith in Christ alone?

Is your faith active and alive?

Is it fruitful unto the purposes of God?

Is it trusting God to the uttermost, even in the hardships?

Is it worshiping, walking, and working with God?

Is your faith obeying God?

Words from Jesus
"In My Father's house are many mansions; if *it were* not *so,* I would have told you. I go to prepare a place for you. And if I go and prepare a place for you, I will come again and receive you to Myself; that where I am, *there* you may be also. And where I go you know, and the way you know' " (John 14:2-4).

Lesson 2: God's Wrath Against Humanity
Romans 1:18-32

Day One: **Read** Romans 1:18-32

Memory Verse: "For since the creation of the world His invisible attributes are clearly seen, being understood by the things that are made, even His eternal power and Godhead, so that they are without excuse..." (Romans 1:20).

Last week's lesson concluded with the revelation of God's righteousness. In contrast, this week's lesson begins by exposing man's depravity and their eternal need for a righteousness that can only come from God. After establishing God's righteousness, Paul gets right to the point. He exposes our need for God. Paul will identify and define humanity's immoral condition for the next three weeks ending with Romans 3:20.

Today's passages are broken down into two sections. Paul establishes the foundation of the guilt of all Gentiles in Romans 1:18-23. He wraps it up by looking at the results of that guilt and outlining the unavoidable consequences in the remaining verses. Scripture confirms that apart from God's righteousness, we were all doomed, eternally damned, and destined for permanent separation from God. We owe all our thanks to God; He had a better plan. God always had a plan to save you!

1. Christ has won your pardon. Are you confidently looking to Christ alone for your salvation?

2. In Romans 1:18, God's wrath is revealed from heaven against *two* things. What are they?

3. Romans 1:18 reports that men suppress something. What is it?

4. Using a dictionary, define *unrighteousness*.

5. In your own words, define *sin*.

6. What may be known to them according to Romans 1:19?

7. What two invisible attributes of God are found in Romans 1:20?

8. Review Romans 1:18-21. God is angry about man's sin. From each passage, list His reason(s). Be specific.

v. 18

v. 19

v. 20

v. 21

9. With darkened hearts, what were the results in Romans 1:22-23?

   v. 22

   v. 23

10. In Romans 1:24, God gave them up to uncleanness in the lust of their hearts. From the verse, what was the outcome?

11. A life-changing exchange was made in Romans 1:25. Please complete the verse below.

"... who exchanged the _____ _____ _____ for the _____, and _____ and served the _____ rather than the _____, who is blessed forever. Amen."

Lesson 2: God's Wrath Against Humanity
Romans 1:18-32

Day Two: **Research**

I. Using a dictionary, bible dictionary, or concordance, define the following *keywords*.

a. *unrighteousness* v. 1:29

b. *sexual immorality* v. 1:29

c. *wickedness* v. 1:29

d. *covetousness* v. 1:29

e. *maliciousness* v. 1:29

II. Read the following *key phrases*.

suppress the truth v. 18 – literally to prevent someone from doing something by restraining or hindering—*to prevent, to hinder, to restrain, to keep from.* From *The Theological Lexicon of the NT*, we find the following detailed explanation. *"It is in this sense that according to Romans 1:18, human* **godlessness and unrighteousness** *'hold the truth' captive in the chains of unrighteousness. By not adhering to the truth from the heart and not submitting their conduct to it, they somehow* **shackle the divine truth and hold it in check** *[emphasis added]."*

manifest in them v. 19 - a literal translation would be *"God is clearly known in them."* The primary sense of the word is visible. *The Greek-English Lexicon of the NT* states, *"the meaning as 'clearly known, easily known, evident, plain, clear.'"*

His invisible attributes v. 20 - What are God's invisible attributes? To name a few, He is eternal, immanent, which means in all things. He is omniscient (all-knowing), omnipresent (everywhere at the same time), and omnipotent (all-powerful and all-mighty). For clarity read Isaiah 40:26 and Colossians 1:26-17. Record the highlights of God's attributed below.

From Isaiah 40:26 -

From Colossians 1:16-17 -

knew God v. 21 - From *The Greek-English Lexicon of the NT* - "they possessed information about — 'to know, to know about, to have knowledge of, to be acquainted with, acquaintance.' They were acquainted with God; they knew Him. Therefore, it was not ignorance that leads to their self-destructive and depraved behavior; instead, it was a blatant rebellion."

glory of the incorruptible God v. 23 - literally they exchanged the expectation, opinion, reputation, honor, glory of the imperishable and immortal God, who is the great I AM, into an image after themselves.

receiving in themselves the penalty of their error v. 27 - Our text reports that those choosing to engage in a perverse sexual activity receive the "due penalty" of their error. The Greek for "due penalty" is not talking about an unusual punishment from God. Instead, it emphasizes that those engaging in such sin will reap the consequence which is natural and logical to their actions. As God's created beings, His image-bearers, we cannot violate the natural use of our bodies without consequences. The word "use" in verses 26 & 27 is *chrēsis* in Greek. The meaning of "use," according to the *Dictionary of Biblical Language: Greek New Testament and The Greek-English Lexicon of the NT* is "*sexual function, sexual use.*" Note: It is crucial to understand there is no mention of "orientation, bent or inclination" in the word's original meaning.

Even though people excuse sin and push their "orientation, bent, or inclination" positions today, Paul merely stated God's position, and here's that point. All the "offenders" were using (and use) their bodies outside the natural order and sexual function as designed by God. We cannot violate our bodies' natural use and then blame God for the shameful or painful results. All sin has consequences. Paul said, "...the wages of sin is death..." (See Romans 6:23.) The end result is always the same. If we remain unrepentant, we will die in our sin. We'll experience spiritual death in addition to our natural death. Lest we forget, only the Redeemed of God will inherit His kingdom.

God gave them over v. 28 - This is a judicial term relating to judgment and the dispensing or administration of justice. In Greek, the term is used for handing over a prisoner to his sentence. When men consistently abandon God, there are painful consequences.

Record Azzariah's message to Asa from 2 Chronicles 15:2 -

debased mind v. 28 - From *The Greek-English Lexicon of the NT*, debased - *adokimos* means *"pertaining to not being in accordance with what is right, appropriate, or fitting—'not fitting, what should not be done, bad.'"*

righteousness judgment of God v. 32 - A literal translation is right or just judgment of God. God's righteous judgment is justifiable, justified, legitimate, defensible, supportable, rightful; admissible, allowable, understandable, acceptable, and reasonable. *The Amplified Version* of Romans 1:32 states, "Although they knew God's righteous decree and His judgment..." Read and record Ecclesiastes 12:14 below. Take note, God knows our deepest secrets, and His judgment is always righteous. "What will God bring?" Underline your answer.

Record Ecclesiastes 12:14

deserving of death v. 32 - literally worthy of death - earning a penalty. *The Greek-English Lexicon of the NT* states the contextual meaning of the word *deserving*. *"Bringing up the other beam of the scales; bringing into equilibrium; therefore, equivalent." It* speaks of bringing balance and justice. In sinful disobedience, spawned by pride and arrogance, they rebel against God, disregarding Him altogether. Dr. Joe Miller, a professor of Applied Theology and Leadership at Southern California Seminary, has said: "So too, as God's creation, we cannot violate the natural use of our bodies and then blame God for the resulting sickness, disease, or emotional suffering which are the natural consequence [due penalty] of ignoring His instruction manual."

Record Psalm 14:1

Record Galatians 6:7-8, paying particular attention to God's word concerning sowing and reaping.

Lesson 2: God's Wrath Against Humanity
Romans 1:18-32

Day Three: **Receive**

Prayerfully Review Romans 1:18-32

Memory Verse: "For since the creation of the world His invisible attributes are clearly seen, being understood by the things that are made, even His eternal power and Godhead, so that they are without excuse..." (Romans 1:20).

In today's lesson, we come into agreement with God concerning our moral and depraved condition when we defiantly declare: "There is no God!"

1. We concluded our lesson from Day One by recording the words of Romans 1:25. Please review the verse.

2. In your own words, define *lie*.

3. Although you may not know it, telling a *lie* is more profound than merely stating a falsehood. It speaks to motive and the intentions of the heart. The underlying intent is to deceive or mislead. Reviewing Romans 1:25, what *lie* have they believed?

4. Although man's chief purpose is to glorify God, they believed a lie instead. We find the progression of a lie in Romans 1:18-25. In your opinion, which verse from these passages most clearly identifies the beginning of their decline? Record the verse below.

5. Review Romans 1:18-25. *Truth* cannot be changed, but it can be held down, stifled, and ignored. Take note. These actions don't change or alter "truth." However, over time, our understanding can be hardened, which leads to darkness. If we go this way, our blindness is self-imposed. Have you held down, stifled, or ignored God's truth?

6. Ignoring the truth of God never ends well. Prayerfully review Romans 1:18-25. From these verses, we can see that "blind ignorance and willful defiance" is not bliss, but rather, it's amoral, chaotic, and destructive. Over time, rejecting God always leads to the same place – anarchy! The evidence of the moral collapse of society is captured in Romans 1:26-27. Although we suppress, ignore, and reject God's truth, the truth remains unchanged. God always responds with justice to our vile passions and perverse lifestyles. God never changes, and our ignorance won't sway His righteous dealings with us. From Romans 1:26-27, how did God justly respond?

   a. Who does God's Word call out first? For what? Be specific.

b. Who does God's Word call out next? For what? Be specific.

c. What were they filled with as a result? Be specific.

7. Romans 1:28 shows that our actions produce consequences. Due to their downward spiral and moral decline God gave them over "to something and for something." What?

8. See Romans 1:29-31 below. It has been stated that if a man's thoughts are devoid of God, his life is characterized by not *just a touch of unrighteousness* but a *fullness of unrighteousness* that touches every part of his life. Paul's explosive list confirms that thought. Notice the order in which they're listed. (See similar verses in Mark 7; Galatians 5; 1 Timothy 1; and 2 Timothy 3.)

"And just as they did not see fit to acknowledge God any longer, God gave them over to a depraved mind, to do those things which are not proper, being filled with all unrighteousness, wickedness, greed, evil; full of envy, murder, strife, deceit, malice; **they are** [emphasis added] gossips, slanderers, haters of God, insolent, arrogant, boastful, inventors of evil, disobedient to parents, without understanding, untrustworthy, unloving, unmerciful;..." (Romans 1:28-31) NASB.

a. In essence, Romans 1:28 reveals that in their prideful failure to acknowledge God, He gave them over to their depraved minds to do those things which are not proper, leading to four (NASB) and five (NKJV) general vices. List the vices from Romans 1:28.

1._____

2._____

3._____

4._____

5._____

b. The next five acts/actions are related to envy:

1._____

2._____

3._____

4._____

5._____

c. As a result, *they are*:

1._____

2._____

3._____

4._____

5._____

6._____

7._____

8._____

9._____

10._____

11._____

12._____

13._____

Note: Although translations vary, God's opinion does not. Twelve (12) characteristics are listed in the NASB and thirteen (13) are listed in the NKJV.

9. Could there be a more depressing and sinful list? Humanity has sunk to the lowest level! Rejection of God always leads down the trail of moral decline and spiritual darkness. It should be well-received into our spirits that a willful or deliberate rejection of the divine revelation of God hardens the heart to the point that the rebel even delights in the sinfulness of others. Could we get any lower than this?

Read, receive, and record Paul's closing words from Romans 1:32 below. As you record the passage, take time to pray for the lost. Many are far from God; perhaps someone in your family falls into that category. God will hear your prayers from heaven and answer! Here's His faithful promise.

"...if My people who are called by My name *will humble themselves, and pray and seek My face, and turn from their wicked ways* [emphasis added], then I will hear from heaven, and will forgive their sin and heal their land" (2 Chronicles 7:14).

Romans 1:32

Lesson 2: God's Wrath Against Humanity
Romans 1:18-32

Day Four: **Reflect**

Review Romans 1:18-32

Memory Verse: "For since the creation of the world His invisible attributes are clearly seen, being understood by the things that are made, even His eternal power and Godhead, so that they are without excuse..." (Romans 1:20).

Ignoring God does not absolve us of sin or protect us from its painful consequences. Quite the contrary. When we live as though there is no God, or He is dead, we deceive ourselves. As we discovered yesterday, the outcome is predicted in Romans. Essentially, Paul cautions against willful disobedience. He says it leads to painful consequences, presently and in the life to come.

In today's lesson, you are invited to examine some of the scripture's most significant passages concerning homosexuality. Theologians overwhelmingly agree that Romans 1:26-27 provide the most explicit teaching on homosexuality in the NT. God has spoken clearly! He has not kept us in the dark concerning sin, including deviant sexual behavior.

1. Since the fall, man has had a natural bias against God. Throughout history, they have pushed against God, and many have rejected Him altogether. The original sin was wanting to be God rather than submitting to God. There is a natural order of decline when we deny the existence of God. When we stubbornly reject the divine revelation of God, the outcome is always the same. Read Ephesians 4:18. What is hardened?

Noted theologian R.H. Mounce made the following observation. *"To turn from the light of revelation is to head into darkness. Sin inevitably results in a darkening of some aspect of human existence. In a moral universe, it is impossible to turn from the truth of God and not suffer the consequences. Ignorance is the result of choice. People who do not "know" God are those who have made that choice.* ***Understanding God requires a moral decision, not additional information*** *[emphasis added]."*

In Romans 1:20, Paul reminds us that "all we need to know God has been revealed." Therefore, we are without excuse if and when we reject the divine revelation of God. Before we move forward, prayerfully review Romans 1:20 again.

2. Read Romans 1:24. Notice that God gave them over to their sin. The essence of divine judgment is God allowing people to go their own way. In the Apocrypha, (Wisdom of Solomon 11:16) Solomon stated "One isi punished by the very things by which he sins."[1]

Additionally, *The Twentieth Century New Testament* commentary concludes "God has abandoned them to impurity. Moral degradation is a consequence of God's wrath, not the reason for it. Sin inevitably creates its own penalty."

Since the beginning of God's recorded dealings with humanity, His divine judgment has ultimately permitted people to go their own way and reap the consequences. Because they have rejected Him, He has let their sin escalate to self-destruction. Some examples would be Pharaoh, Judas, and the residents of Sodom and Gomorrah, etc. Read Psalm 81:11-12.

    a. What did God's people refuse to heed, and what would they not have?

---

1   Mounce, R. H. (1995). *Romans* (Vol. 27, p. 81). Nashville: Broadman & Holman Publishers.

b. What were the results? Summarize Psalm 81:12 below.

Let's look at the condition of man and the painful consequences when they chose to turn from God's truth. Once the moral compass is lost, chaos, perversion, lawlessness, and the general loss of self-respect of humanity follows. And what was the outcome? The degrading of their bodies with one another. It has been said since man is made in the image of God, there is a very real sense that if God goes, so goes man. There is an element of natural decline. When we dishonor God, eventually we dishonor ourselves. When God becomes nothing, over time we become even less.

3. Romans 1:26-27 provide the clearest description of homosexuality in all of scripture. In these two passages, **God defines exactly what homosexuality is**! When God speaks, our opinion is irrelevant! Record God's definition from Romans 1:26-27 below.

v. 26

v. 27

4. An examination of Romans 1:26-27 from *The Amplified Bible* might prove beneficial.

Romans 1:26 "For this reason God gave them over to degrading and vile passions; for their women exchanged the natural function for that which is unnatural [a function contrary to nature], 27 and in the same way also the men turned away from the natural function of the woman and were consumed with their desire toward one another, men with men committing shameful acts and in return receiving in their own bodies the inevitable and appropriate penalty for their wrongdoing" (Romans 1:26-27).

5. Homosexuality is condemned through both testaments. (See Leviticus 18:22; 20:13; and 1 Corinthians 6:9-10.) Review Romans 1:26-27 and list the five primary reasons the verses records that "God gave them up to vile passions..."

   1.

   2.

   3.

4.

5.

The end of Romans 1:27 reads *"the due penalty of their error."* ESV. A correct understanding of these words shapes the overall passage. We see that God has said those choosing to participate in "homosexual activity" receive the "due penalty" of their error. Note: the error was man's, not God's. The Greek for the "due penalty" is not talking about a special punishment from God. It emphasizes that those "engaging in such sin" will reap the consequence which is natural and logical to their actions.

In *The Expanded Translation of The Greek New Testament*, its author, Dr. Stephen Wuest, made this observation about *the due penalty of their error*. He concluded they "received in themselves that retribution which was a necessity in the nature of the case because they deviated from the norm." Dr. Wuest is speaking of God's norm, which is the nature of God's divine creation.

Based on a careful examination of these verses, we wrap up today's lesson with these thoughts.

HIV/Aids and other sexually associated diseases and illnesses are **NOT** a punishment from God. These natural occurrences do **NOT** reflect God's judgment or vengeance upon any individual.

Our takeaway from Romans 1:27 is this. When men and women chose to violate the Creator's design, it leads to the body's natural corruption. By analogy, when a person violates a product's intended design, they void the manufacturer's warranty. Let's look at three random examples.

a. My Conair blow dryer. The user's manual states, "Do not submerge in water." Doing so would destroy the blow dryer and could cause electrocution. The warning is not only written in the instruction pamphlet. It's illustrated by a drawing of a bathtub and an industry-wide **Do Not Symbol** ⊘. If I decide to test the waters, so to speak, I'm responsible for the outcome. They have clearly stated, "Do Not Submerge In Water." If I submerge it, my warranty is null and void, and it might kill me in the process.

b. My Infiniti Q50. My car requires Premium Unleaded Fuel – only. The owner's manual states it, my gas tank lid states it, and the window sticker on my car alerted me to this fact before I purchased it. That means regular unleaded fuel will not do! If I choose to buy regular unleaded fuel, and my car is sluggish or worse, won't run, it's on me. I violated my warranty when I ignored the owner's manual (manufacturer's instructions) by purchasing a lower octane fuel. Any adverse effects are my responsibility, financial and otherwise.

c. My female Chihuahua. Lily suffers from bouts of pancreatitis. According to my veterinarian, "She will require a special diet for the remainder of her life." When I feed her other things, she gets sick. The consequences are not only painful for her but for me too. They cost me mental anguish because I have to watch her suffer, and it costs me in the pocketbook as well. Veterinary care is expensive.

So too, as God's creation, we cannot violate the natural use of our bodies and then blame God for the resulting sickness, disease, or emotional suffering, which are the natural consequence or the *due penalty* of ignoring His instruction manual.

6. Not to make light of such a serious topic, but when, if ever, have you willfully violated God's law? What were the natural consequences? You are invited to share. Be discreet.

Lesson 2: God's Wrath Against Humanity
Romans 1:18-32

Day Five: **Respond**. Review Romans 1:18-32

Memory Verse: "For since the creation of the world His invisible attributes are clearly seen, being understood by the things that are made, even His eternal power and Godhead, so that they are without excuse..." (Romans 1:20).

2 Peter 1:3 states, "...as His divine power has given to us all things that pertain to life and godliness, through the knowledge of Him who called us by glory and virtue..." We owe all our thanks to God. The redeemed will spend eternity with Jesus, but this verse says much more. It begins here and now by pursuing godliness and modeling Christ for the benefit of the gospel. Peter assures us that "God has given us the power to accomplish all things that pertain to life and godliness through the knowledge of Him." The verse speaks of an intimate relationship with Jesus that manifests, sustains, and perfects godly living - presently. Sadly, a review of Romans 1:29-31 highlights a stark contrast. These verses identify the vices or characteristics which flowed from the lives of those that God gave over to their debased minds. Let's review the passage from the NASB.

Romans 1:29-31 "...being filled with all unrighteousness, wickedness, greed, evil; full of envy, murder, strife, deceit, malice; they are gossips, slanderers, haters of God, insolent, arrogant, boastful, inventors of evil, disobedient to parents, without understanding, untrustworthy, unloving, unmerciful;..." NASB

Note: The brief definitions below were taken from *The Greek-English Lexicon of the NT* as they specifically pertain to Romans 1:29-31. Look closely. Although the words appear similar, they all have a unique meaning and purpose within the passage. Remember, every word in the Bible is God-breathed and has a divine purpose.

I. ♥ <u>Heart-Check For Today</u>.

Below you will find twenty vices from Romans 1:29-31. First, read through the list. Next, select **seven (7) vices** through which God has mercifully delivered you. Those chosen should involve a heart-change, an awakening, or an overcoming of unrighteousness or adversity. Before you make your selection, ask yourself this question. "Has God mercifully delivered me in this area?" Be honest and make it personal.

For your answer, you may either 1.) share a brief testimony of God's deliverance or heart- change concerning your selected characteristics, or 2.) list a scripture that confirms the word's meaning. As you pray through this list, consider whether or not any of these characteristics are present in your life today.

    a. *wickedness* - the lack of moral uprightness.

    b. *greed* – the insatiable desire to have more.

    c. *evil* - the quality of wickedness, evil, badness with the implication of that which is harmful and damaging.

d. *full of envy* - a state of ill-will toward someone because of some real or presumed advantage experienced by such a person—envy, jealousy.

e. *murder* - to deprive a person of life through an illegal, intentional killing.

f. *strife* - conflict resulting from discord and rivalry.

g. *deceit* - to deceive by using trickery and falsehood.

h. *malice* - disposition leading one to habitually engage in malicious acts; intended or intending to do harm.

i. *gossips* - one who habitually engages in gossip - a gossiper - a tale-bearer - one who whispers with the intent to harm.

j. *slanders* - to speak evil of.

k. *haters of God* - a person with great disdain, dislike, and/or contempt for God - prejudiced against God.

l. *insolent* - someone who thinks up schemes or plans of action.

m. *arrogant* - pertaining to being pretentious or showy; proud with the desire to impress —arrogant, haughty, contemptuous.

n. *boastful* - showing pretentious pride, one who is pretentiously proud and given to bragging about it.

o. *inventors of evil* - they think of plans, actions, or schemes of doing evil.

p. *disobedient to parents* - children who willfully fail or refuse to obey their parents.

q. *without understanding* - pertaining to a lack of capacity for insight and understanding; senseless, foolish.

r. *untrustworthy* - pertaining to not being bound or not regarding oneself as bound by any covenant or agreement—'not keeping a promise, not abiding by an agreement.

s. *unloving* - pertaining to a lack of love or affection for close associates or family—without normal human affection, without love for others.

t. *unmerciful* - they are without understanding, disloyal, unloving, and merciless - having no compassion for someone whom it is within your power to punish or harm.

II. Read Romans 6:15-23 and fill in the blanks from verses 22 and 23 below.

"But now having been set _____ from _____, and having become slaves of God, you have your fruit to _____, and the end, _____ _____ . For the wages of sin is _____, but the _____ of God is eternal _____ in _____ _____ Our Lord."

III. Get alone with God. Enter into His presence for a time of prayer and confession as you reflect upon Romans 1. Remember, there is no time better spent than time with God.

Words of Jesus
"...The time is fulfilled, and the kingdom of God is at hand. Repent, and believe in the gospel"
(Mark 1:15).

Lesson 3: God's Righteous Judgment - The Jews And The Law
Romans 2:1-3:8

Day One: **Read** Romans 2:1-3:8

Memory Verse: "Or do you despise the riches of His goodness, forbearance, and long-suffering, not knowing that the goodness of God leads you to repentance?" (Romans 2:4)

1. Being the chosen people of God did not exempt the Jews from God's judgment, as many must have thought. Paul is straightforward with God's indictment concerning judgment. Record Paul's warning message of Romans 2:1 below.

2. Review Romans 2:1. Paul lists two reasons to support his claim of man's inexcusable guilt concerning judgment. What are the reasons? Be specific.

   1.

   2.

3. Self-righteousness puffs us up and tempts us to judge. Read Matthew 7:2. What did Jesus teach about self-righteous judgment from His radical Sermon on the Mount?

4. Read Romans 2:2. For clarity on judgment, prayerfully read Psalm 96:13. Paul's inspired message concerning judgment was also straightforward. By what standard will God judge? Review Romans 2:2 and record the words or phrases that support your answer below.

5. Notice in Romans 2:1, the opening word is *"Therefore."* Paul is drawing a conclusion. Read Romans 2:3. What do you think Paul means by the phrase, *"practicing such things and doing the same"* in verse 3? What things could Paul be referencing?

6. Read and review Romans 2:4. What leads you to repentance? Be specific.

7. Read Romans 2:5 and answer the following questions.

   a. Using a bible, bible dictionary, or concordance, define *impenitent*.

   b. What were they treasuring for themselves? Be specific.

8. Read Romans 2:6-7. Who will render, how, and what will we receive? Be specific.

   Who?

   How?

What?

9. Romans 2:8-11 summarize the plight of those who are self-seeking and disobey God's truth. List the consequences from each verse below.

v. 8

v. 9

10. Review Romans 2:10-11 and answer the following questions.

a. From Romans 2:10, what three things are promised to those who *"work what is good?"*

1._____

2._____

3._____

   b. Complete Romans 2:11 concerning God's partiality.

For there is _____ _____ with _____.

11. Read and review Romans 2:12-13. Who will be justified?

12. Read Romans 2:14 and answer the following. The Gentiles do something by nature and become something as a result. What?

   1.

   2.

68 · Anne Nicholson

13. From Romans 2:15, what two ways were the work of the law shown in the Gentiles? As a result, their thoughts accomplished two things. What were they?

The work of the law was shown:

a._____

b._____

And between themselves, their thoughts:

c._____ or _____

14. Prayerfully complete Romans 2:14-16 below.

"...for when Gentiles, who do not have the law, by _____ do the things in the law, these, although not having the law, are a law to_____, who show the work of the law _____ in their_____, their _____ also bearing witness, and between themselves *their* thoughts _____ or else _____ them in the day when _____ will _____ the _____ _____ _____ by Jesus Christ, according to my _____."

(Romans 2:14-16).

Lesson 3: God's Righteous Judgment - The Jews And The Law
Romans 2:1-3:8

Day Two: **Research.**

I. Using a bible, bible dictionary, or concordance, define the following *keywords*.

a. *inexcusable* v. 2:1

b. *repentance* v. 2:4

c. *unrighteous* v. 2:8

d. *indignation* v. 2:8

e. ***tribulation*** v. 2:9

f. ***abhor*** v. 2:22

g. ***blasphemed*** v. 2:24

h. ***circumcision*** v. 2:25; 2:26; 2:27; 2:28; 2:29; 3:1

i. ***transgressor*** v. 2:27

II. Read the following *key phrases*.

according to truth v. 2:2 - From *The Greek-English Lexicon of the NT,* "('in truth,' 'upon truth,' and 'according to truth') pertaining to being a real or actual event or state—*'actually, really.'* " The literal meaning is linked to the OT rendering of the truth, which is firm, and therefore solid, valid, and binding. God's divine truth identifies what is true and is the standard by which all truth is measured. Because understanding "truth" is so significant, prayerfully complete Psalm 96:13 below.

"For He is coming, for He is coming to judge the earth. He shall judge the world with _____, and the peoples with His _____" Psalm 96:13

judgment of God v. 2:3 - references a *universal judgment* for all men - the Jews and the Gentiles. It is the divine judgment of a holy and righteous God, the creator of all things, the great I AM. In keeping with its usage in most NT passages, the judgment focuses on the decision maker's ability and worthiness to judge. In these NT passages, generally speaking, the judgment is unfavorable and bears the sense of condemnation. The judgment is either an action or the result of an action. Note: In this verse, it is a result of an action.

Psalm 50:6 (Record the last phrase)

Psalm 75:7

storing up for yourself wrath v. 5 - The term references the results of the rejection of God's merciful offer of forgiveness. The author of Hebrews suggests unrepentant sin perpetuates the accumulation of more of God's wrath. That's wrath upon wrath. Rejection of God always comes at a premium price, and the results are eternal. Prayerfully read Hebrews 10:26-30. What important facts are revealed in Hebrews 10:30?

Hebrews 10: 30

according to my gospel v.16 - Paul was protective of the gospel. He had determined to know nothing among them except Christ and Him crucified. His heart burned after the gospel. It was his calling, his passion, and his greatest joy to preach and teach Christ crucified. It is your personal gospel, as well. As a believer, the gospel is good news to you! Read and record the words of 1 Corinthians 2:2 below.

1 Corinthians 2:2

having a form of knowledge and truth in the law v. 20 - The Jews had the law. They possessed knowledge of what could be known through the words of the Torah. In other words, they had a witness of God's written law – the Commandments. Paul is quick to remind them that with divine favor comes privilege as well as responsibility. Their self-righteousness was an abuse of their esteemed position and birthright in God's overall plan. They, "The Jews, God's chosen" - were to be a "witness or testimony" in the land that God lived! Overall, they were to be a blessing to all others.

Instead, they possessed a "form or embodiment of knowledge and truth" that propelled them to self-aggrandizement rather than humble service to others. They fell short. Their posture reflects all believers who misuse or squander the knowledge of God's truth to serve their own baser instincts rather than serving God. It's a heart issue. They were selfish rather than selfless. Read and complete Philippians 2:3-4 below.

"*Let* nothing *be done* through _____ ambition or _____, but in _____ of mind let each esteem _____ _____ than _____ . 4 Let each of you look out not only for his _____ interests, but also for the interests of others" (Philippians 2:3-4).

circumcision is that of the heart v. 29 - According to Paul, the only true circumcision is that of the heart. It's a work of the Spirit, for only the Holy Spirit can change a heart. The base meaning of *circumcision* is to cut around, to make incisions. Biblically speaking, the significance of circumcision is linked to the OT. It was a precondition, sign, and seal of participation in the covenant with Abraham. It was also a sign of confession that they belonged to God. It was an outward sign of an inward manifestation of God. It indicated they were set apart to love God fully – with their whole being – inside and out. God had cut away the old heart and made it new in Him. The covenant blessings promised by God accompanied it. Prayerfully read Deuteronomy 30:6.

Who bears the responsibility for the work?

What is the final benefit?

the faithfulness of God v. 3:3 - the faithfulness of God has never been dependent upon man's acceptance or rejection of Him. He is faithful even when we are not. His plan will be accomplished. Nothing stops the faithful purposes of God.

"Let us hold fast the _____ of *our* _____ without wavering, for _____ who _____ *is* _____" (Hebrews 10:23).

Lesson 3: God's Righteous Judgment - The Jews And The Law
Romans 2:1-3:8

Day Three: **Receive.** Review Romans 2:1-3:8

The Jews were as guilty as the Gentiles. Paul, a former Pharisee of Pharisees, calls them out! No one better understood their foolish religious pride and selfish ambitions than Paul. Review Romans 2:17-24 and answer the following questions.

1. Read Romans 2:17-18. Paul begins by listing five conditional clauses which describe the Jews. Record the conditional clauses below. Verse 17 begins, "Indeed you are called a Jew,…"

1. ex: rest..._____

2. _____

3. _____

4. _____

5. _____

2. The Jews were puffed up with national pride and boasted of their unique relationship with God. However, their self-confidence had lead them off course. Paul makes four accusations in Romans 2:19-20? List them below.

1. _____

2. _____

3. _____

4. _____

3. In Romans 2:20, we discover the root of their false sense of pride. What was it?

4. Read Romans 2:21-23. Paul makes a series of statements and asks five (5) questions. Record the correlating question to each statement below.

v. 21. You, therefore who teach another,_____

v. 21. You who preach that a man should not steal,_____

v. 22. You who say, "Do not commit adultery,"_____

v. 22. You who abhor idols,_____

v. 23. You who make your boast in the law,_____

5. Read Romans 2:24-25 to discover the results of their national pride and self-righteousness. Their circumcision was profitable if the law was kept. But, what happened if the law was not kept? Record your answer from the appropriate words of Romans 2:25.

6. ♥ <u>**Heart-Check For Today**</u>.

The truth about circumcision is revealed in Romans 2:25-29. Paul exposes their hearts through these compelling verses. As you read these passages and answer the corresponding questions, consider the condition of your heart. It's good to ask the Holy Spirit to show us the truth about ourselves in light of God's Word. King David was a man after God's heart. He routinely asked God to purify him and expose the condition of his own wicked heart. As you read and complete King David's request from Psalms 139:23-24 below, let it be your prayer for today.

Search me, O God, and know my _____; Try me, and _____ my _____; And see if *there is any* _____ way in me, And _____ me in the way _____" (Psalm 139:23-24).

7. Turn to Genesis 17:9-14 to review God's original plan for circumcision, which was the sign of the covenant. God's covenant is irrevocable. He will be faithful to His pledge throughout eternity. We can see, however, from the words of Paul that the Jews had lost sight of the true meaning and purpose in the rite of circumcision. Read and record the important facts of Genesis 17:9-11.

v. 9

v. 10

v. 11

8. Read Romans 2:25-29. From Paul's admonition to the Jews, we can clearly see they had linked their prideful hope for eternity to their birthright as descendants of Abraham, rather than on faith accompanied by their obedient and worshipful relationship with God. They were trusting in their ties to Abraham rather than God. In the space below please outline Paul's **important words of warning** to the Jews from each verse.

v. 25

v. 26

v. 27

v. 28

v. 29

9. For clarity and reinforcement, please answer the following questions from Romans 2:25-29.

From v. 25 -

    a. When is circumcision profitable?

    b. What makes it an uncircumcision?

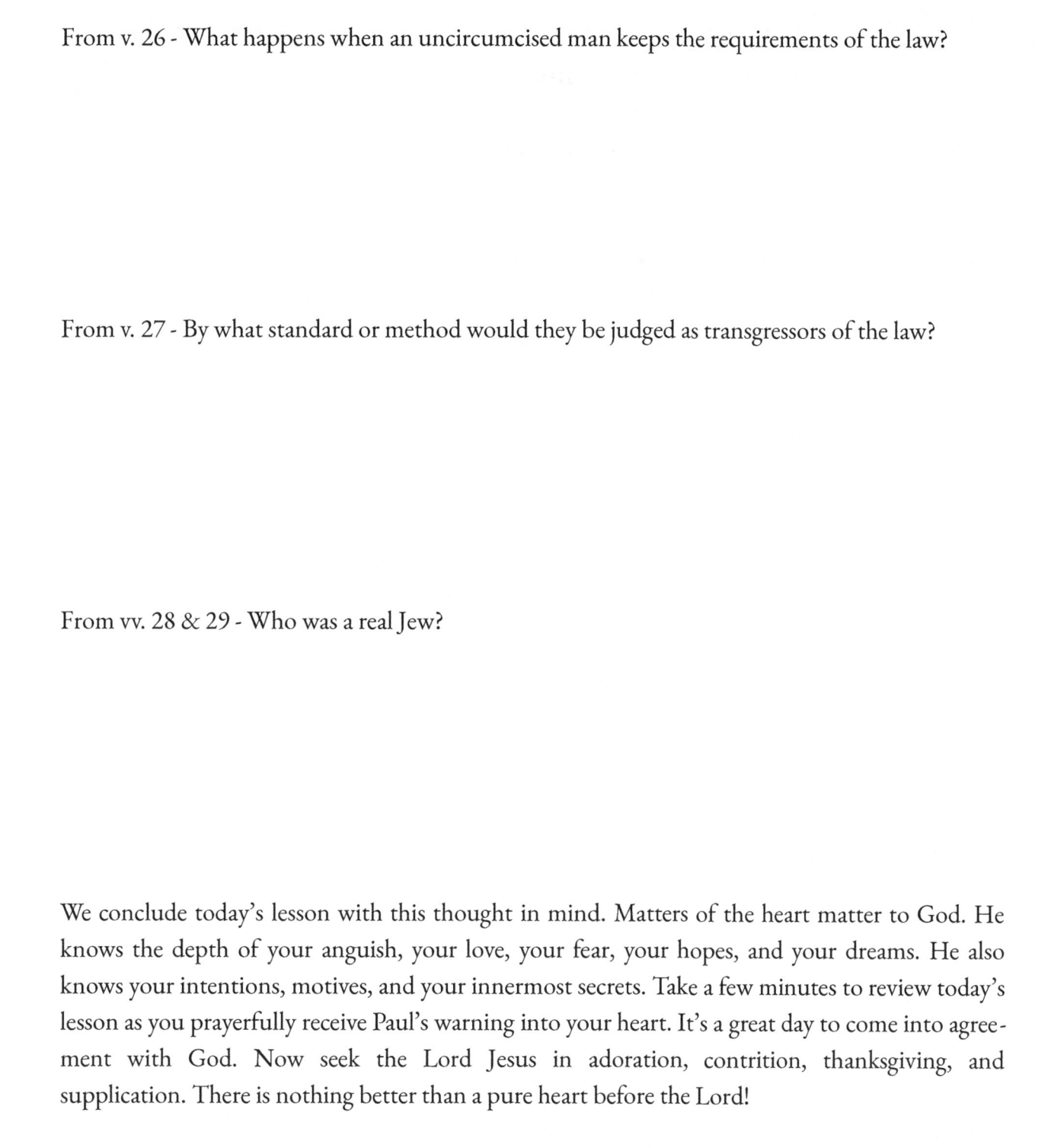

From v. 26 - What happens when an uncircumcised man keeps the requirements of the law?

From v. 27 - By what standard or method would they be judged as transgressors of the law?

From vv. 28 & 29 - Who was a real Jew?

We conclude today's lesson with this thought in mind. Matters of the heart matter to God. He knows the depth of your anguish, your love, your fear, your hopes, and your dreams. He also knows your intentions, motives, and your innermost secrets. Take a few minutes to review today's lesson as you prayerfully receive Paul's warning into your heart. It's a great day to come into agreement with God. Now seek the Lord Jesus in adoration, contrition, thanksgiving, and supplication. There is nothing better than a pure heart before the Lord!

Lesson 3: God's Righteous Judgment - The Jews And The Law
Romans 2:1-3:8

Day Four: **Reflect.** Prayerfully review Romans 2:1-3:8.

1. Being a Jew was no guarantee of eternity. That's precisely why Paul's inspired words posed an important question to the Jews in Romans 3:1 What was it? Record the verse below.

Romans 3:1

2. Paul states an advantage. He provides a chief reason in Romans 3:2. What was it?

3. Thinking biblically, why was this reason important?

4. For greater insight into their rich heritage, read and complete Paul's words from 2 Timothy 3:15 below.

"...and that from _____ you have known the _____ _____, which are able to make you _____ for _____ through _____ which is in Christ _____" (2 Timothy 3:15).

5. Read Romans 3:3-4. Will the unbelief of some alter the faithfulness of God? Yes___ or no____?

6. Despite man's unbelief and faithlessness, God is eternally faithful. He is the same yesterday, today and forever. Record your favorite verse concerning the faithfulness of God. You are invited to share.

7. Review Romans 3:3. In this verse Paul contrasts the Jews sinfulness with the faithfulness of a covenant-keeping God. Do you have a personal testimony of God's faithfulness when you were perhaps not so faithful?

8. Read Romans 3:4 and complete the verse below.

82 · Anne Nicholson

"Certainly not! Indeed, let God be_____ but every man a _____. As it is written: *"That You may be _____ in Your words, And may overcome when You are_____"* (Romans 3:4).

9. From Romans 3:4, Paul quotes the memorable words of King David's confession in Psalm 51:4. Here, Paul reminds the Jews of God's faithfulness. These are passages that would have been familiar to the Jews. These words serve as a reminder that King David knew the faithfulness of God. He knew of God's faithfulness to His righteous character, even in judgment. He is a just God! God has also repeatedly affirmed His faithfulness in scripture. Read Exodus 34:5-7 to discover how God has identified **Himself** and cast a spotlight on His faithful dealings with humanity. Record the words and phrases from Exodus 34:6-7, which convey His character.

v. 6

v. 7

10. Read Romans 3:5-8. In verses 5-6 Paul poses a human argument that our unrighteous conduct could enhance the righteousness of God, but quickly refutes it. What words indicate that Paul quickly refutes humanity's errored argument and thought? Be specific.

11. Turn to Day Two, Part II, *"according to the truth."* Notice that you recorded the powerful words of Psalm 96:13 in that exercise. To reinforce the meaning of the verse, please review it and paraphrase the verse below. You are invited to share your thoughts concerning the coming righteous judgment of God.

12. Paul concludes his indictment of the Jews in Romans 3:7-8. He vehemently refutes the thought that good comes from evil. What judgment does he pronounce on those who slanderously reported and affirmed that thought? The answer is embedded in the verse. Record the final phrase of Romans 3:8 below.

Lesson 3: God's Righteous Judgment - The Jews And The Law
Romans 2:1-3:8

Day Five: **Respond**. Prayerfully Review Romans 2:1-3:8

Memory Verse: "Or do you despise the riches of His goodness, forbearance, and long-suffering, not knowing that the goodness of God leads you to repentance?" (Romans 2:4).

Today it's your turn. The goodness of God inevitably leads sinners to repentance. Complete the following exercises as you pause to examine the critical elements of the riches of His goodness. Remember these very riches - from the beginning of recorded time - have led multitudes of sinners to repentance. We owe all our thanks to God! That same goodness, forbearance, and long-suffering will continue to lead sinners through that narrow gate of repentance until the day of His coming. That should give you great comfort. As you work through these exercises, take the time to prayerfully remember those who are living under the lie of the enemy while falsely assuming there is no God. Perhaps even in your own family, lost souls need Jesus. Respond accordingly and take those petitions to Jesus in prayer.

Below is a list of the riches of His goodness: Note: This is an incomplete list. As you journey through Romans, you are encouraged to consider the limitless goodness of God's riches in Christ Jesus. You will be thoroughly blessed.

1. His glory - Read and record Psalm 19:1. What declares His glory? Circle your answer.

Psalm 19:1

2. Who is His mystery? Read Colossians 1:27 and record the last phrase of the verse.

Colossians 1:27

3. The purpose of the mystery of Christ is revealed through Ephesians 3:8-12. Where are the riches found? What is accomplished through Christ?

4. The glory of the resurrection – Read 1 Peter 1:3-4 and answer the following questions.

   a. What type hope do we have through the resurrection?

   b. What adjectives are used to describe our inheritance?

c. How is our inheritance kept? Record 1 Peter 3:5 below.

5. The glory of His grace - Read Ephesians 1:3-6 and complete the following statements.

v. 3 Blessed *be* the God and Father of our Lord Jesus Christ, who has:

v. 4 just as He chose us in Him before the foundation of the world:

v. 5 "...having _____ us to adoption as _____ by Jesus Christ to _____, according to the good pleasure of His _____,

v. 6 "...to the praise of the _____ of His _____, by which He made us _____ in the Beloved."

6. Believers enjoy the magnificent surety of forgiveness. Peace of mind and a clear conscience are gifts from God. Read Ephesians 1:7. In whom do we have God's forgiveness?

7. Our pardon is profound! To grasp the full assurance of His pardon, read Hebrews 10:22-23. Why is our faith unwavering?

8. His presence - Read Exodus 33:14 and Psalm 16:11. Which of the two selected verses grabs your heart? Why?

9. His presence - You are invited to share your favorite new testament verse which speaks to your heart concerning the glory of His presence.

10. As we conclude this week's study, prayerfully consider the goodness of God which leads to repentance. Make a list below of friends, neighbors, colleagues or family members who do not know Jesus. Would you make a commitment to pray for their salvation as you study through Romans? You have an opportunity to imitate Paul's love and concern for those outside the family of faith. You are invited to ask a sister in Christ to hold you accountable to your pledge.

Friends:

Neighbors:

Colleagues:

Family Members:

Words of Jesus
"Then He said to His disciples, 'The harvest truly is plentiful, but the laborers are few. Therefore pray the Lord of the harvest to send out laborers into His harvest' " (Matthew 9:37-38).

Lesson 4: The Depravity of Mankind
Romans 3:9-20

Day One: **Read** Romans 3:9-20

Memory Verse: "They have all turned aside; They have together become unprofitable; There is none who does good, no, not one" (Romans 3:12).

The past three lessons have contrasted humanity's unrighteousness in light of God's righteousness. His searchlight has exposed not only our sins, but the depth of the evil in man's heart. Remember, God sees everything! Nothing - absolutely nothing - escapes the watchful eye of God. Next week, Paul will sum up our sinful condition by saying: "For all have sinned and fall short of the glory of God..." (Romans 3:23).

In today's lesson, Paul will bring God's indictment against humanity front and center. There is no doubt about it. The Gentiles are guilty as well as the Jews. That means we're all as guilty as guilty can be! Thank God we have a remedy – His name is Jesus. His righteousness becomes yours when you believe. How merciful is our God? He is a just God who loves us. He will not leave us in our hopeless state – condemned and destined to be separated from Him throughout eternity. We owe all our praise and thanks to God. Yes, He had a plan. It was always God's plan to save us, and that includes you!

1. Paul opens today's scripture with a question. Read Romans 3:9 and answer the following questions.

   a. Who is Paul referring to as *we*?

   b. Who is Paul referring to as *they*?

2. To ensure their understanding, Paul answers his own question. What does Paul conclude about the Jews and the Greeks? Record Paul's inclusive summary statement from verse 9.

3. Underline the last five words of verse 9 from question 2 above.

4. Define *sin* in your own words.

5. Paul begins Romans 3:10 with the most common reference or introduction to old testament scripture. What does he say? Record the words:

6. Complete Romans 3:10-12 below.

"There is _____ righteous, no, _____ _____;

There is none who _____;

There is none who _____ after _____.

They have all _____ _____;

They have together _____ _____;

There is none _____ _____ _____, no, not one."

7. List the words from the blanks above. Look closely. Do you see a natural pattern of decline?

8. It is evidenced from these select words that our departure from God is linked to our progression of sin. What were the painful results? Record the last phrase of Romans 3:12 below.

9. Read Romans 3:13-14 and answer the following questions.

    a. What was an open tomb?

b. What about their tongues?

c. What was under their lips?

d. What fills the mouth?

10. Read Romans 3:15-16 and answer the following questions.

a. What was swift to shed blood?

b. What two things are in their ways?

11. Read Romans 3:17-18 and answer the following questions.

   a. What had they not known?

   b. What was not before their eyes?

12. Paul concludes his indictment in Romans 3:19-20.

   a. What was the purpose of the law in verse 19? Be specific.

   b. Record Romans 3:20 below.

Lesson 4: The Depravity of Mankind
Romans 3:9-20

Day Two: **Research**

Memory Verse: "They have all turned aside; They have together become unprofitable; There is none who does good, no, not one" (Romans 3:12).

I. Using a bible, bible dictionary, or concordance, define the following **keywords**.

a. *unprofitable* v. 12

b. *tomb* v. 13

c. *deceit* v. 13

d. *swift* v. 15

e. *destruction* v. 16

f. *misery* v. 16

g. *knowledge* v. 20

II. Read the following **key phrases.**

none who understands v. 11 - From *The Greek-English Lexicon of the New Testament* we find our definition of **understands**: *"to be able to understand and evaluate—'to be able to comprehend, to understand, (to be) intelligent, (to have) insight, intelligence.'* Man lacked understanding, they could not comprehend the truth of God. Not because God's truth had been withheld or because they lacked opportunity, but rather their lack of understanding was rooted in foolish pride, rejection, and rebellion. Read Ephesians 4:18 and answer the following.

a. What happened to their understanding?

b. What were they alienated from?

c. What was in them and why?

seeks after God - v. 11- God promised that if we seek Him we will find Him. (See Deuteronomy 4:29.) Sinful rebellion steeped in pride prompted man to worship other gods. We chose to be God instead of bending our knee to the true and living God. It was the original sin. False religions have long satisfied man's desire to escape God, to avoid God, rather than seek after God. It is interesting to note; however, the desire to seek Him is a direct result of God's work in your heart. What a privilege we enjoy as believers. God not only loves us - He woos us! Jesus is always waiting for you! Seek Him, and you will find Him. Read Proverbs 8:17. Prayerfully record the first phrase of the verse below.

turned aside v. 12 - "turned aside" means to lean in the wrong direction. One theologian likened its original meaning to describe a solider running the wrong way or deserting. Referencing *The Greek-English Lexicon of the New Testament*, to turn aside, "to avoid," to no longer put one's trust or confidence in someone—'to turn away from (God). In essence, to veer off path, to venture off course, to swerve."* From the beginning of time, man's natural inclination has been departure from God's way while seeking after their own. Again, that was the root of the original sin. What is sin? At its core it's disobedience to God. Our definition is: *any failure to conform to the moral law of God in act, attitude, or nature*. So that we're clear concerning sin, that would include our words, actions, and deeds, as well as our motives and intent. Complete Isaiah 53:6 below.

"All we like _____ have gone _____; we have turned, every _____, to his _____ way; And the Lord has laid on Him the _____ of us all."

an open tomb v. 13 - Literally an open grave, which would expose or emit the decay, disease, and stench of the deceased to passersby. Metaphorically speaking, "Their open throats, like tombs" exposed the condition of man's heart by allowing others (passersby) to smell the stench and decay of their cold dead hearts. Read Matthew 12:34 below. What does Jesus say about the origin or our words? Record the phrase below.

Note: Sin has not changed, nor will it. Sin is sin, and salvation is still salvation; furthermore, God's plan has not changed. Dr. Warren W. Wiersbe, author, and theologian stated: "There is no difference in the great message of Romans—no difference in sin (Romans 3:22–23) or salvation (Romans 10:12–13). God has regarded both Jew and Gentile as under sin that He might, in grace, have mercy upon all" (Romans 11:32).[2]

destruction and misery v. 16 - *Destruction* in this verse references *ruin* which means disintegration, decay, and despair. *Misery* in this verse references wretchedness, hardship, and distress. These words define the ways, direction, and manner in which they lived. Generally speaking, destruction and misery were their way of life – it was a lifestyle! Verse 16 describes the character of sin and how it responds. For reinforcement and clarity, prayerfully read Isaiah 59:7-8.

way of peace v. 17 - The phrase is not referencing an inner peace or serenity. From this passage, "way of peace" is linked to man's natural bent toward conflict and strife with people and nations. The word "way" references the course or the direction to that peace. What peace? **Peace with God and *peace* with others.** From the *Theological Dictionary of the NT*, "way" is - *the narrow path trodden by those who have gone before.* Take note. There is a specific "*way of peace*" and saints before us have found it. Verse 17 describes the conduct of sin. Read and record Isaiah 57:8 below.

fear of God v. 18 - Biblical fear of God is a two-fold revelation linked to the nature and character of God. First, revelation of God brings awe and wonder to the hearts of man. Next, that revelation is accompanied by a healthy, reverent fear of violating God's holy nature. In other words, to know Him is to love Him, to reverence Him, and to obey Him. Complete Proverbs 9:10 below.

"The _____ of the _____ is the beginning of _____,

And the _____ of the _____ One is _____."

---

2 Wiersbe, W. W. (1992). *Wiersbe's expository outlines on the New Testament* (p. 370). Wheaton, IL: Victor Books.

justified in his sight v. 20 - Literally "righteous in his [God's] sight." From *The Dictionary of Biblical Languages with Semantic Domains: Greek (New Testament) by James A. Swanson,* we find that justified means *"to put right with, justify, vindicate, declare righteous, i.e., cause one to be in a right relationship - declare righteous - to have right standing..."* (in the sight of God). Additionally, from *The Greek-English Lexicon of the New Testament,* we find the following words concerning the word justified. *"It is the act of clearing someone of transgression—'to acquit, to set free, to remove guilt, acquittal - from all (the sins).'"*

God is the only source of righteousness, because it can only come from Him. This is a legal or forensic term in Greek and it appears 30 times in the book of Romans. We will examine righteousness thoroughly as we journey through Romans. Read and complete Isaiah 45:8 below. Pay special attention to "righteousness." Who created it?

"Rain down, you _____, from above, And let the skies pour down _____; Let the earth open, let them bring forth _____, And let _____ spring up together. I, the _____, have _____ it."

Lesson 4: The Depravity of Mankind
Romans 3:9-20

Day Three: **Receive**. Review Romans 3:9-20

Memory Verse: "They have all turned aside; They have together become unprofitable; There is none who does good, no, not one" (Romans 3:12).

1. We begin today's lesson with Paul's summary statement of Romans 3:9. According to Paul, both the Jews and Greeks "are all under sin." Paul will substantiate his claim as we move through the lesson. With wisdom and accuracy, he reaches back into the old testament for confirmation through the inspired words of the psalmist. In so doing, he eloquently proves humanity's depraved condition by highlighting their predisposed temperament, natural bent, and inclination to sin. As we shall see, they were enslaved and dominated by sin. Incidentally, anyone who lives apart from Christ's righteousness remains the same. Read and record Romans 3:9 below.

2. Read Psalm 14:1-3 and record the highlights from each verse.

v. 1

v. 2

v. 3

3. Now read and record the ***similar words and phrases*** from Psalm 53:1-3. Pay special attention to the last phrase of verses 1 and 3. Be sure to include these words in your answer.

v. 1

v. 2

v. 3

4. Review Romans 3:10-18 below. Underline the words "none or not one" and circle the words "all, together" and "their/they" in these passages. These inclusive words reveal the nondiscriminatory evil of humanity's sin and rebellion. How many times does Paul use each group of words?

none; not one _____ all; together; their/they _____

As it is written:

"There is none righteous, no, not one;
There is none who understands;
There is none who seeks after God.
They have all turned aside;
They have together become unprofitable;
There is none who does good, no, not one."
"Their throat is an open tomb;
"With their tongues they have practiced deceit";
"The poison of asps is under their lips";
"Whose mouth is full of cursing and bitterness."
"Their feet are swift to shed blood;
Destruction and misery are in their ways;
And the way of peace they have not known."
"There is no fear of God before their eyes."

5. Review Romans 3:10-18. These verses expose and confirm their guilt. They also serve as an indictment of their character, conversation, and conduct. In your opinion, which verse(s) speak to the following:

their character:

their conversation:

their conduct:

6. As you can see, turning aside from God affects the whole of our lives, including our character and conduct. A careful review of Romans 3:10-18 confirms that departure from God leads to worthless, useless, and unprofitable lives. Sadly, their turning from God was not an accident or oversight. It was a deliberate and intentional act. Consequently, Bible scholars agree that not one of their actions was honorable, "no, not one." We must remember every decision we make is linked to a consequence. As you consider the words of Romans 3:10-18, have you ever intentionally turned aside from God? Have you ignored God and gone left when He said, "Go right?" Jonah did! If so, what were the painful consequences, and how did God restore you?

7. God has given you one body with which to glorify Him or not. As a child of God, Acts 1:8 calls you to be a witness - His witness. Our words, actions, and deeds should exalt Him and never cause others to question His authenticity, power, authority, or very existence. Remember, question #6 above reveals that turning aside from God affects the whole of our lives. Sadly, many Romans had

veered off the path and were not living to the glory of God. Paul's inspired words highlight the evidence of its effects on the whole of the body.

Review Romans 3:10-18 and locate the verse(s) linked to the appropriate body parts and record how they were used for evil rather than glorifying God.

a. the throat_____

b. the tongue_____

c. the mouth_____

d. the lips_____

e. the feet_____

f. eyes_____

8. ♥ <u>**Heart-Check For Today**</u>.

A life lived to the glory of God looks quite different. It bears fruit for Him. Read and record the following passages. Let God's word wash over you, renew your mind, and encourage your faith as you prayerfully receive His truth into your heart and spirit. May you be strengthened for the Romans journey! Read John 15:1-8 and Colossians 1:10. From John 15, record the following verses.

John 15:4-5

John 15:8

Lesson 4: The Depravity of Mankind
Romans 3:9-20

Day Four: **Reflect**. Review Romans 3:9-20

Memory Verse: "They have all turned aside; They have together become unprofitable; There is none who does good, no, not one" (Romans 3:12).

1. When we abide in Christ, we avoid two specific consequences. They are found in Romans 3:12. Read and identify these specific consequences when we reject God. What are they?

   a.

   b.

2. In Romans 3, Paul calls attention to the tongue. Prayerfully read James 3:9. The verse says the tongue was created with the express purpose of praising our Creator. Romans 3:13 speaks metaphorically about the tongue, mouth, and lips, as well as their collective capacity for destruction. Yet, they do not work alone. Please note. The tongue and its counterparts do not speak on their authority, either. Jesus taught that the tongue speaks from another source. Thinking biblically, what is the source or root of verbal communication? Cite a passage below to support your answer.

3. If you're acquainted with God's Word, the study of the tongue is not new. James spoke forcefully about its many uses for both good and evil in James 3. At the Holy Spirit's inspiration, James linked many NT sins to the tongue, calling out slander, criticism, judgment, and blasphemy, to name a few. In Romans 3:13, Paul calls out deceit or lying specifically.

   a. Thinking biblically, who is the "Father of Lies"? _____
   b. Review John 8:44 and complete the last sentence of the verse below.
   "...When he speaks a lie, he _____ from his own _____, for he is a liar and the father of it.
   c. The last phrase of Romans 3:13 states, "The poison of asps [cobras, vipers] is on their lips." Thinking biblically, what does this imply? Why is this so dangerous?

4. Reformed theologian R. C. Sproul stated the following. "The fracturing of truth is characteristic of fallen man and sets man apart from God who speaks no lie." Read and record Hebrews 6:18 below. Note: The NLT has a beautiful rendering of this passage.

Hebrews 6:18

5. Romans 3:14 identifies two verbal products of the mouth: bitterness and cursing. Both are by-products of fallen humanity, and both are birthed in the heart of man. Originally, *cursing* meant *wish or petition*, and it appears in our text as a quote from Psalm 10:7. The intent was to speak harm or injury upon a person or people; it meant evil and is still evil. The curse was intended to be immediate or contingent upon particular circumstances. *Full of cursing* does not necessarily imply packed full or crammed full to overflowing. In the *Greek-English Lexicon of the New Testament*, we find the following " *'...their mouths are full of bitter curses' (Romans 3:14). It may be difficult or even meaningless to speak of a person's mouth as being 'full of bitter curses,' but one can often say 'they are constantly cursing harshly' or '... speaking heavy curses' or '... constantly uttering harmful curses.' " In this passage, full of cursing speaks to the frequency of the cursing. Bitterness in this passage* references *the open, public expression of emotional hostility against one's enemy.* Complete Psalm 10:7 below.

"His _____ is full of _____ and _____ and _____; Under his tongue *is* _____ and _____."

6. In your own words, define the word *hostile*.

7. As you thought about the word "hostile," did words like unfriendly, unkind, bitter, malicious, vicious, antagonistic, aggressive, confrontational, or belligerent come to mind? If so, you grasped the word's meaning. Hostile behavior exposes fallen men who push against God, their fellow man, and, ultimately, themselves. Nothing good ever comes from a life that rejects God, and the *way of peace* will never be found. Sadly, the results not only impact their lives presently, but they will also have eternal consequences. Read and complete Romans 6:23 below.

"For the wages of sin *is* death, but the gift of God_____

_____."

8. Read Romans 3:15. Thinking biblically, what is meant by "their feet are swift to shed blood"?

9. All over the world, there is a profound lack of reverence for God. We see it every day through violence and hatred, which spawns more violence and hatred. Evil perpetuates evil. Today, life has no value. Subsequently, to kill someone is nothing; there is no remorse, no regret, no humility, and no shame. A sense of entitlement and self-aggrandizement is rampant. People are out of con-

trol. Anarchy is present when God is not. Let's look at that again. Where God does not rule, anarchy prevails!

Paul understood the consequences of rejecting God. We see the sad evidence in the verses before us. Romans 3:10-18 paint a vivid picture of their demise. Verse 18 reminds us, "There is no fear of God before their eyes." Their spiritual condition is apparent; they are void of God! They had no holy fear and no submission. That's always a heart issue. Their hardened hearts had ruined their vision, and they were blinded. Regretfully, they could not see God before them or remember Him as God the Father, the great I Am, the true purveyor of mercy and justice. Read 2 Peter 3:9 and answer the following questions.

   a. Who is not slack, and what does it concern?

   b. Instead, what is He towards us?

   c. What is He unwilling to accept and why?

10. Please record your favorite verse about submission or reverence for God. You are invited to share.

Lesson 4: The Depravity of Mankind
Romans 3:9-20

Day Five: **Respond**. Review Romans 3:9-20

Memory Verse: "They have all turned aside; They have together become unprofitable; There is none who does good, no, not one" (Romans 3:12).

1. Thinking biblically, what was the purpose of the law? Please record a verse in support of your answer.

2. Who received the oracles of God through Moses? As a reminder, review Romans 3:2.

3. How have the Gentiles received the works of the law? As a reminder, read and record Romans 2:15 below.

4. Complete Romans 3:19-20. "Now we know that whatever the _____ says, it says to those who are under the law, that every _____ may be stopped, and all the _____ may become _____ before _____. Therefore by the deeds of the law no_____ will be _____ in His sight, _____ _____ _____ _____ is the _____ _____ _____."

5. Review Romans 3:19 and answer the following questions:

   a. What do you think is meant by "every mouth may be stopped."

   b. Thinking biblically, why do you think this was necessary?

6. Look at the last phrase of Romans 3:20. The law makes sin known. The law itself is not sin, and it is not evil. Simply stated, its divine purpose is to reveal God's holy standard so that you may come to the knowledge and understanding that you have sinned through your failure and inability to meet God's holy standard. As a preview of coming weeks, **read and paraphrase** Paul's words regarding sin and the law from Romans 7:7.

7. Thanks to God, the law makes us conscious of sin. Have you recently become aware of sin in your life? If so, you are invited to share. Please include these two answers in your testimony. 1). When and how the revelation of sin came to your conscience? And 2). How did the working grace of God redeem you through the revelation?

8. ♥ <u>**Heart-Check For Today - Coming Into Agreement With God**</u>.

The time has come for your response. Prayerfully consider the following statement. You are being redeemed every day by the grace of God and for His glory. He loves you entirely and desires to bring you into the right relationship with Him. Believers battle between the spirit and the flesh. It's a spiritual battle. We are at war. To complicate matters, we also have free will. We can choose to come into agreement with God or not. Our unreasonable delay often brings painful consequences. It is always best to agree with God quickly as you acknowledge and confess your sin.

Have you ever resisted the impulse to submit to God? Yes _____ or No ___?

Is it possible you're resisting Him now? Yes _____ or No _____?

Words from Jesus
"Then He said to her, 'Your sins are forgiven' " (Luke 7:48).

Lesson 5: Through Christ Abraham Is Justified By Faith
Romans 3:21-4

Romans Road Map: Before you move ahead, let's review what you've studied. Lesson 1 introduced you to Paul, his mission, and the purpose of Romans. In Romans 1:16-17, you discovered the theme or thesis for the book of Romans. Every verse in Romans will build, expand, and support that central theme. What was it? Mainly this: God wanted you to know and understand that the "just will live by faith!" Faith in Him, in Christ alone.

In lessons 2, 3, and 4, Paul exposes humanity's unrighteousness in light of God's righteousness. Paul painted a vivid portrait of man's sinful struggle and deep-rooted bent, inclination, or predisposition for evil rather than good. You discovered that every human is evil and falls short of the glory of God. According to Paul, none is good, not even one! Just when you are overwhelmed with the reality of your sinful condition and eternal plight, salvation comes. Faith explodes in you, and hope and victory reign! You owe all your thanks and praise to God. From the foundation of the world, He had a plan! He sent Jesus! He planned to save you by giving you His righteousness. The most extravagant gift you're ever received is your salvation through faith in Christ alone!

Lessons 5 - 6 will highlight God's grand plan for salvation through faith in Christ alone.

Salvation comes to all who believe and call upon the name Jesus. As you already know, life is full of twists and turns, and today's Romans journey takes a sweet bend in the road and points us toward a hill called Calvary. But before Paul takes us there, his inspired words reach back to the old testament to show you the beginning of how "the just have lived by faith!"

Day One: **Read**. Prayerfully read Romans 3:21-4.

Memory Verse: "For what does the Scripture say? 'Abraham believed God, and it was accounted to him for righteousness' " (Romans 4:3).

Read Romans 3:21-24 and answer the following questions:

1. From Romans 3:21, what is revealed and how is it witnessed? Be specific.

What?

How?

2. From Romans 3:22, what is extended through faith in Jesus Christ, and to whom? Be specific.

What?

To Whom?

3. In Romans 3:22, Paul says all believers are the same. Why is there no difference? Record your answer from verses 23-24 below.

   v. 23

   v. 24

4. Review Romans 3:21-24. These verses support Paul's claim that he is not ashamed of the gospel. This points us back to the theme of the book of Romans. For review, please read and record Romans 1:16-17 below.

5. Read Romans 3:24-26 and answer the following questions:

Justification came *by something* and *through someone*.

Justification by:_____

Justification through:_____

6. Complete the following passages from Romans 3:25-26.

"...whom God set forth as a _____ by His blood, through _____, to demonstrate His _____, because in His forbearance _____ had _____ _____ the _____ that were previously _____, to demonstrate at the present time His _____, that He might be _____ and the _____ of the one who has _____ in _____."

7. The righteousness that comes from God provides what man can never achieve, attain, or accomplish. It was always beyond our reach. This righteousness is rooted in what God did, not in what people may do. It is freely received and never earned. It wholly depends on faith, not labor or award-winning works and deeds. God justifies sinners, the ungodly, not those who believe they are good or merely do good. In fact, He demonstrated His love for you through death on the cross when you were yet a sinner. (See Romans 5:8.) That's what makes the gospel such "good news" because, according to Paul, not one of us is good!

Read Romans 3:27-28 to discover Paul's leading question and profound statement. Please answer the following questions.

    a. From Romans 3:27, where was boasting abolished?

    b. From Romans 3:28, "Therefore...." how was man justified?

8. To complete today's lesson, fill in the blanks from Romans 3:29-31 below. In this passage, Paul asks and answers a series of questions that end with a summary statement that explains the law's relationship to faith.

"Or *is He* the _____ of the _____ only? *Is He* not also the God of the _____? Yes, of the Gentiles also, since *there is* _____ _____ who will justify the _____ by _____ and the _____ through _____. Do we then make void the _____ through faith? Certainly not! On the contrary, we _____ the law" (Romans 3:29-31).

Paul concludes Chapter 3 by pointing out the only method by which God justifies man: by faith and faith alone. That has always been God's way of setting people right with Himself. In verse 31, Paul asks and answers an important question. Is the law null and void because of faith? His answer confirms that faith establishes the law rather than abolishing it. Faith is the essential component of God's divine plan. God never intended that we earn our righteousness. He knew it would be humanly impossible.

Even on your best days and through your best efforts, your offerings would be tainted by the human condition called sin. That's what the law does. It reveals sin. To sum it up, faith confirms and supports the law in the sense that faith fulfills all of the law's obligations. You need not worry; all that was required in the law has been satisfied through your faith in Christ. It's always been by faith alone, in Christ alone!

Lesson 5: Through Christ Abraham Is Justified By Faith
Romans 3:21-4

Day Two: **Research**.

Memory Verse: "For what does the Scripture say? 'Abraham believed God, and it was accounted to him for righteousness' " (Romans 4:3).

I. Using a bible, bible dictionary, or concordance, define the following *keywords*.

a. *justified* v. 24

b. *redemption* v. 24

c. *propitiation* v. 25

d. *forbearance* v. 25

e. *imputes* v. 6, 8

II. Read the following **key phrases**.

being justified freely v. 24 - literally having a right standing before God at no cost to you. Note too, that justification has not been earned. Read and record Romans 5:1 below.

by His grace through the redemption v. 24 - Literally *His grace* is the means of God's unmerited, undeserved favor through redemption which is the loosening, release, liberation, or freedom from sin, slavery, and bondage. Read Ephesians 1:7 below. What do we have according to the riches of His grace? Be specific.

propitiation by His blood, through faith v. 25 –

propitiation - From the *Greek-English Lexicon of the New Testament*, *"propitiation is essentially a process by which one does a favor to a person in order to make him or her favorably disposed."* From this definition, *being favorably disposed* means *to have a right or reconciled relationship with God - according to God; to have right standing; and to be declared not guilty for all sins, past, present and future.* Christ was the only suitable sacrifice to meet the holy standard set by God.

by His blood – *"His blood"* references Jesus' blood, which was spilled on Calvary to atone for humanity's sins. Therefore, His death was sufficient, suitable, and acceptable in the eyes of God. Through Jesus' death on Calvary, God's wrath against humanity was fully satisfied - forever. The blood of Jesus is the only means by which man is reconciled to God. He is the way, the gate, the door! Remember, the forgiveness of sins always required the "shedding of blood" or a blood sacrifice. The old testament sacrifices were a foreshadow of Christ's atoning work on Calvary.

through faith – You instantly received *right standing* before God the moment you came to faith. *That would be the moment you believed that Jesus died for your sins.* That *right standing – Jesus' righteousness* - was immediately credited to your spiritual account. You didn't earn it, and you can't buy it! You were saved by grace through faith. That means it was God's good pleasure to extend His unearned, unmerited favor to you. The results? You came to faith – you believed, and your life changed instantly – including your eternal destiny. Alas, you believed in Jesus, and you were saved. It's a spiritual transaction from start to finish. *The Greek-English Lexicon of the New Testament has defined faith as follows.* "Faith is to believe to the extent of <u>complete trust and reliance — 'to believe in, to have confidence in, to have faith in, to trust in</u> [emphasis added]." God had given us His definition of faith in His Word. Read and record Hebrews 11:1 below.

Abraham had this faith. "And he [Abraham] believed in the Lord, and He [God] accounted it to him for righteousness" (Genesis 15:6). Simply stated, although Abraham was as guilty as guilty can be (as we all are/were), the moment he believed in the Lord, God imputed Jesus' holy righteousness to Abraham. From that moment, though his sins were as scarlet, God washed them white as snow! Abraham enjoyed *right standing* before God all the remaining days of his life and throughout eternity.

just and the justifier v. 26 – He (God) is wholly righteous and the only one who could provide the means of grace by which you received right standing (righteous standing) before Him. God is the creator of the law, and He is bound to the law's righteous and just standards. God is the *justifier*. As the justifier, He spares you but not at the expense of His integrity. That is never compromised.

His righteousness is always maintained and preserved. Read Romans 8:33 to discover the "just one" who "justifies" you as well. Record the last sentence of the verse.

justified by faith v. 28 - You obtain right standing because you believe in Jesus Christ for salvation. The book of Romans contains no less than 18 passages which speak to justification by faith. Read Romans 3:22; 3:24; 3:28; and 9:30. Complete Romans 10:9-10 below.

"...that if you _____ with your mouth the Lord Jesus and _____ in your _____ that _____ has raised _____ from the dead, you will be saved. For with the _____ one

_____ unto righteousness, and with the _____ _____ is made unto salvation" (Romans 10:9-10).

justifies, justified, justification - Speaks of your righteous standing before God. Romans 10:17 explains the event, circumstance, or occurrence of this divine spiritual transaction. Paul highlights the occurrence of faith, which is the spiritual awakening that leads to and accompanies salvation. Romans 10:17 affirms that faith is ignited by hearing the truth of God. When you respond in agreement, your heart is changed. It is circumcised. The old is cut away and made new. You become a new creature, hidden with Christ in God. Justification is always a spiritual work!

Circumcision And Baptism.

In the old testament, being identified with God was linked to a covenantal, ceremonial rite known as circumcision. **Circumcision** was an outward testimony or expression of an inward manifestation or work of God. It signified to the world that an internal spiritual work had occurred. There had been an awakening, spiritual enlightenment, a revelation, or life-changing understanding that they belonged to God. It symbolized the awareness, presence, and total reliance upon God for saving faith. Remember, the old testament saints lived and died in faith, looking forward to the deliverance that would come through the promised Messiah.

Presently, we look back at the evidence of faith passed and reach forward, by faith, in anticipation of His second coming and the hope of our promised resurrection. All of our hope is in Christ alone.

We, too, have an expression for this marvelous spiritual work. On this side of the cross, believers celebrate **baptism**. It is an outward expression of an internal spiritual work or manifestation of God. It testifies to the world that you belong to God. It says that you are identified with God. Baptism declares to the world that you are a child of God. It affirms that you believe in Christ alone for your salvation. Even today, a circumcised heart still belongs to God - faith is still faith - and you are declared righteous because you believe. Read Romans 10:17. How does faith come? Be specific.

justified by works v. 2 - literally made right by an act, deed, or doing. These words seem to imply that you are made right by your performance. However, we know that is not the case.

Justification rests wholly in what Christ has done. It has always been about what Jesus has accomplished on your behalf instead of what you could contribute. God does not need your help in the work of salvation. He desires your belief in Him, in Christ alone. Remember, from start to finish, that salvation is a spiritual work of God. Read and complete Galatians 2:16 below.

"...knowing that a man is not _____ by the_____ of the law but by _____ in Jesus Christ, even we have _____ in Christ Jesus, that we might be _____ _____ _____ in _____ and not by the _____ of the law; for by the works of the law no flesh _____ _____ _____" (Galatians 2:16).

by faith; through faith v. 30 - Paul is speaking of universal faith. The same faith saves both Jew and Gentile. The expression *"by faith"* emphasizes the *means, mechanism, or the agency of grace by which men are saved.*

Faith was essential to Israel's salvation. It is essential to yours, too, because we know that there is no salvation apart from faith in Jesus. Unbelieving Israel did not have faith. They merely had works and works alone have never saved anyone.

The expression ***through faith*** emphasizes that system or process. It is the system or process through which one participates in what God is saying or doing.

That faithful participation is always expressed through the process of coming into agreement with God. Simply stated, you hear His word. agree with it, and live by it. You learn it (hear it and receive it), you love it (agree with it), and you live it (empowered by His spirit, you submit to God, and you hold yourself accountable to His Word for right/righteous living). Read Galatians 3:24 and answer the following questions.

   a. Therefore, what was the law?

b. What was the law's purpose?

c. Why?

accounted to him for righteousness v. 3 - literally credited to him as right standing. *Credited* means *imputed to, attributed to, ascribed to you.* This verse implies that there is a debt to be paid. Abraham's debt was satisfied or paid in full because He believed God; therefore, Christ's righteousness was imputed, attributed, credited, or ascribed to him. Not because of anything Abraham accomplished or could ever achieve. Righteousness was imputed to Abraham solely because he believed God's Word and responded in his heart accordingly.

Read and record James 2:23

Read and record Galatians 3:6

Lesson 5: Through Christ Abraham Is Justified By Faith
Romans 3:21-4

Day Three: **Receive**. Prayerfully read Romans 3:21-4.

Memory Verse: "For what does the Scripture say? 'Abraham believed God, and it was accounted to him for righteousness' " (Romans 4:3).

Background: You cannot study faith without reaching back to its roots. Questions one and two will provide background information concerning Abraham and faith, which will enrich your study in Romans. Why? Because Abraham believed God, and biblical faith was born. (See Romans 4:3.)

One day, thousands of years ago, Abraham heard the voice of God. He was not looking for God, yet God found Him, and His purposes were fulfilled. Abraham was the human vessel through which God chose to reveal His salvation plan and its standards to humanity. When Abraham believed God, humanity's standard for faith was established and recorded. The same faith, like Abraham's, still saves sinners and reconciles them to God.

Faith is faith, and it will never change. It is the means of grace by which God has saved sinners in the past, and until the mountains melt like wax, this means of grace will continue. We owe all our thanks to God! He never changes, nor will His standard for faith. Faith began before the foundation of the world, but its written story beings in Genesis 12.

1. Read Genesis 12:1-9 and fill in the blanks. Note: God changed Abram's name to Abraham in Genesis 17.

a. Abraham had to _____ his country and family. v. 1.

b. God promised to make Abraham a great _____. v. 2.

c. God promised to _____ those who blessed him, and _____ those who _____ him. v. 3

d. God promised "in you [Abram] all the families of the _____ shall be _____." v.3

e. Abram was _____ years old when he _____ from Haran. v. 4

f. Then Abraham took _____, his wife and _____, his brother's son and they departed..... v. 5

g. Abraham passed through the land to the place of _____..... And the _____ were in the land. v. 6

h. "Then the Lord _____ to Abraham and said, 'To your _____ I will give this _____.' " v. 7

i. And there he built an _____ to the Lord who had _____ to him. v. 7

Note: Abraham worshiped for the first time. It was the first act of worship in the Promised Land. In so doing, Abraham made a confession of faith, and established worship. At Shechem, Abraham publicly declared his unwavering faith in God's promise.

j. And he _____ from there to the mountain east of _____, and he pitched his tent *with* Bethel on the west and _____ on the east; there he built an _____ to the Lord and _____ on the _____ of the _____. v. 8

k. So Abram _____ going on still toward the South. v. 9

2. Abraham pleased God. He also holds the distinction of being called God's friend. He is the man through which God chose to reveal to humanity that faith matters and is rewarded. Through His dealings with Abraham, God revealed Himself and His constant faithfulness despite Abraham's humanness. Abraham was not perfect, but He worshiped, served, and honored the One who is, who was, and who forever will be.

Abraham is also known as the father of faith and holds the esteemed biblical position of being the recipient of the Abrahamic Covenant. That's significant because through Abraham's seed, the nations were born, including the nation of Israel.

Through Israel, God's chosen people were identified and established. God's covenantal blessings and promises passed through this chosen line from father to son for generations. Despite their humanness and error, God kept them and remained faithful to every promise. The ultimate fulfillment of this Covenant will occur when Jesus establishes His kingdom reign on earth. God will be faithful. Nothing about God has changed or HIs promises. He remains the same yesterday, today, and forever! Read and record Hebrews 11:6 and James 2:23 below.

Hebrews 11:6 -

James 2:23 -

3. Read Romans 4:1-4. Our memory verse comes from these passages. Abraham believed God! What is significant in these passages? Please list the key words or phrases from each verse.

v. 1

v. 2

v. 3

v. 4

4. Prayerfully review Romans 4:1-4.

   a. Was Abraham justified by works? Please circle Yes or No?

b. How was he justified? From Romans 4:1-4, record the verse which identifies Abraham's justification. Please underline one word in the verse that describes Abraham's participation.

5. From Romans 4:4, what happens to him who works?

6. Read Romans 4:5-8 and answer the following questions.

    a. Whose faith is counted for righteousness?

    b. According to David, what "state of being" is experienced by man when God imputes to him righteousness apart from works? Record your one word answer. _____

c. From Romans 4:7-8, complete the following quote:

"_____ are those whose lawless deeds are _____,

And whose _____ are covered; Blessed in the man in whom the Lord shall not _____ _____."

7. Believers are the most blessed people on earth because the question of their sin has been settled forever. Thinking biblically, what does it mean to have your sins covered? What does it mean to you personally?

8. Read Romans 4:9-12.

a. Which verse confirms that Abraham was justified while he was uncircumcised.

b. What did he receive as a seal of the righteousness of the faith which he had while still uncircumcised? Be specific. v. 11 _____ _____ _____
_____

9. Turn to Day Two: Research and review the paragraph under *"by faith; through faith."* In your own words, describe what old testament circumcision meant and represented.

10. Thinking biblically:

   a. What is circumcision of the heart?

   b. The circumcision belonged to whom?

c. How would it respond? Record your favorite verse to support your answer.

11. Review Romans 4:11-12. Several amazing relational statements are made concerning Abraham in these verses. Please answer the following questions:

a. Who is Abraham to you?

b. Who is he to the circumcised?

c. He is also linked to the uncircumcised.

i. What did they do?

ii. Who is he to them?

iii. What did they receive?

12. To conclude today's lesson, please record the beautiful words of Romans 4:12 below.

In summary, Abraham believed God in his heart, and it ignited a visible response. Abraham went! He left his homeland to follow a God that no one knew to an unknown destiny. Abraham was fully persuaded that God would show him the way. When he believed God, His faith journey began, and it continued throughout his life.

It is the same with you. You believed in your heart, and it ignited a visible response. Or did it? Has your life changed? Abraham's did! He abandoned everything to follow God, and he was richly rewarded. He was blessed not just with material blessings and riches but with eternal riches and the esteemed privilege of being called "God's friend," the "father of faith," and the "father of nations" throughout eternity. When Abraham believed God, it laid a foundation of faith that you can trace through the pages of scripture.

Faith is still at work! That same faith that moved Abraham is still actively at work today.

That same effectual call ignited your heart, birthed faith, and saved you! As you close this lesson in prayer, consider the following. It was not Abraham's work, which earned God's favor - it was his faith. As a result of that faith, he worked. He couldn't help but respond in a visible, evidential way. You are called to go and be His witness in the earth, just like Abraham. (See Acts 1:8). He built an altar and worshiped God in the presence of the enemy at Shechem. Remember, Genesis 12:6 revealed that the Canaanites were in the land. May this lesson inspire and challenge you to do the same!

♥ Heart-Check For Today.

13. Abraham's response to God was not only obedient, but it was accompanied by action. For clarity, it's not faith and works, but rather *"faith at work or faith that works."* Abraham's faith worked; it was active and alive to the purposes of God.

In light of that, prayerfully consider the following questions.

How has your faith responded?

Are you worshiping in the land in the presence of the enemy?

Are you living for Christ?

Lastly, are you resting wholly in the grace of Christ's finished work on Calvary?

Take some time to pray through these questions. No written response is required unless you feel compelled to answer. Remember, your faith journey is between you and God! However, If you record a response, you are invited to share.

Lesson 5: Through Christ Abraham Is Justified By Faith
Romans 3:21-4

Day Four: **Reflect**. Prayerfully review Romans 3:21-4.

Memory Verse: "For what does the Scripture say? 'Abraham believed God, and it was accounted to him for righteousness' " (Romans 4:3).

1. Read Romans 4:13-15 and answer the following questions.

   a. From Romans 4:13, through what means was Abraham promised to be heir of the world?

   b. Review Romans 4:14-15. There would be no need for faith if the promise were contingent on your obedience to the law. The promise of Abraham being the heir of the world was not linked to law-keeping, which apart from faith is akin to self-righteous works, but rather it was bound to faith. It was faith-righteousness. Abraham was made righteous because he believed God, not because he worked to keep the law. No human could ever keep the law. According to God's holy standard, which was the law, only Jesus lived a life worthy to be called sinless. Only Jesus kept the law - every jot and tittle - as fully God and man. That was the purpose in His coming, to do for you what you could never accomplish on your own. That is the grace and mercy of God at work on your behalf.

Under what condition would faith become void and the promise made of no effect? Hint: Review the first phrase of Romans 4:14 to discover the answer, and record it below.

2. Review Romans 4:15. What did the law bring about and what was the result?

   What?

   What was the result?

3. In your own words describe the purpose in the law.

4. It has been said that faith is helplessness reaching out in total dependence on God. How beautiful. The responsibility for dispersing faith depends on God, not anything we could ever do or accomplish. We must simply believe. Romans 4:16 begins *"Therefore..."* Generally, *"therefore"* leads to a summary statement but, in this particular instance, the term reaches forward and not backwards. It points to the phrase which links it to grace. Review Romans 4:16 and record the phrase which links *"therefore"* to grace.

5. Review Romans 4:16 and explain how Abraham is your father.

6. Read and complete the following from Romans 4:17-18.

(as it is written, "I have made you a _____ of many _____") in the presence of Him whom he believed—_____, who gives life to the _____ and _____ those things which do not exist as though they did; who, contrary to hope, in hope _____, so that he became the _____ of many _____, according to what was spoken, "So shall your _____ be."

7. Read Romans 4:19 and focus on the things that Abraham did not consider because he was strengthened in faith. Complete the following passages.

a. he did not consider _____ _____ _____

b. he did not consider himself already dead, (since he was about ___ years old),

c. and the deadness of _____ _____.

d. Abraham did not waver at *something* as a result of unbelief. To discover the answer, record the first eleven words (the first phrase) of Romans 4:20 below.

8. From Romans 4:20-21 record the positive results of Abraham's strengthened faith or reliance upon God's promise.

   a. (Abraham) was strengthened in:

   b. (Abraham) was giving:

   c. (Abraham) was being fully convinced:

9. His profound statement of v. 22 links us back to the overarching theme of Romans. Record Romans 4:22 below.

10. For reflection and review, please record Romans 1:16-17 below. Take note. It's the theme verse for the entire epistle.

11. You have examined aspects of God's spiritual work through faith in today's lesson. Do you see that Abraham merely believed, and God strengthened that faith to a fuller measure? How much faith is required? According to Jesus, a small measure is sufficient.

To discover how much faith is required, record Matthew 13:31-32 below. Reflect, dear sisters, on the wonderful works of God and His perfect plan to nourish and grow your faith. May your faith grow like a tree large enough for all the birds of the air to nest in its branches.

v. 31

v. 32

♥ **<u>Heart-Check For Today</u>**.

12. Has your faith been strengthened and encouraged through someone else's story? If so, lay-up some stones of remembrance. Take a few minutes to record your testimony of God's faithfulness. It will strengthen not only your faith but also the faith of others.

Unsure where to start? Consider this. Sometimes our most remarkable growth occurs on the other side of pain, discouragement, or persecution. God doesn't plan it that way, but He uses it to hold us close and strengthen us nonetheless.

Before you begin to share, pray. And, then, remember that through the good times and the bad, a faithful God has held you.

So here's a question to get you started. "How has a faithful God held you?" Begin your story below.

Lesson 5: Through Christ Abraham Is Justified By Faith
Romans 3:21-4

Day Five: **Respond**. Prayerfully review Romans 3:21-4.

Memory Verse: "For what does the Scripture say? 'Abraham believed God, and it was accounted to him for righteousness' " (Romans 4:3).

Before you respond to God's word, let's review and highlight the faith of Abraham. Remember, Abraham's faith matters to us because it mattered to God. His recorded faith has set the standard for all faith to come.

1. For review, read Romans 4:18, which concludes, "So shall your descendants be." This references one of God's original promises to Abraham. What was it? Record Genesis 17:5 below.

2. Abraham knew he and Sarah were too old to have children, nonetheless, he believed God's promise. To fully grasp Abraham's awareness of their hopeless plight apart from God's divine intervention, read and complete Genesis 17:17 below.

"Then Abraham fell on his face and _____, and said in his _____, 'Shall *a child* be _____ to a man who is _____ _____ years old? And shall _____, who is ninety years old, bear *a* _____?' " (Genesis 17:17).

* * *

3. Read Romans 4:20. This verse is significant because it highlights the depth and power of Abraham's faith. Paul says Abraham's faith did not waver. From *The Theological Dictionary of the New Testament,* we find the following explanation concerning "waver." The original word in Greek is

diakrinō. From the verse, Abraham has a divine promise which far exceeds the possibilities of natural fulfillment. He is full of the fact that God will make a reality of this promise. Here the emphasis obviously falls on the unreserved nature of his confidence. He trusts with his whole heart and overcomes everything that might impede this trust. One might almost translate the verse, "He was not inwardly divided …"

At the root of the word's original meaning, we find the essence of "double-mindedness." Yet, we see from scripture Abraham's mind did not wrestle with a conflicting view or opinion. He agreed with God and believed. Paul's inspired words provide a standard of surety that Abraham never quivered; he never flinched, nor did his faith weaken in any measure. Instead, he was resolute and unwavering in his faith. Watch this. Abraham's faith more than prevailed. Romans 4:20 says Abraham's faith "was strengthened." How so? His faith was fully engaged or ignited instantly. It was persuaded, strengthened, and accomplished at the hearing of God's word. (Recall Romans 10:17, "So then, faith comes by hearing and hearing by the word of God.")

His faith was based on God, not human capability or effort. Abraham knew only God could accomplish that which was promised! What did we say? Faith is helplessness reaching out in total dependence on God. Abraham had unwavering hope in God, and his response was profound. What was it? Your answer is found in the next to the last phrase of Romans 4:20. Complete verse below.

"He [Abraham] did not waver at the promise of God through unbelief, _____ _____ _____ _____ _____ giving glory to God,…" (Romans 4:20).

Let's go a little deeper. <u>Biblical faith is confident obedience to God's word despite the circumstances or consequences.</u> Abraham never let his or Sarah's elderly status or the painful reality of their long, childless marriage discourage him. To others, it would have appeared hopeless. But not to Abraham. He heard God's word and believed, moreover he responded. His faith was strengthened. Abraham's hope was not in himself or Sarah, but rather it was trusting in the One who promised. His faith compelled him to look beyond what the eye could see or what his heart could feel. Faith is never linked to what we can *see in reality*, or what might *seem logical in our minds*, or *makes us feel warm and fuzzy*. The inspired definition declares that "faith is the substance of things hoped for, the evidence of things not seen" (Hebrews 11:1).

Give thanks to God! You are a descendant of Abraham because you have believed. Read and review Paul's concluding statements found in Romans 4:22-25 and answer the following questions.

4. From Romans 4:22-23. What words were not written for Abraham's sake alone?

Note: For questions 5 – 8, review Romans 4:20-25

5. Abraham's faith has impacted you.

   a. Pause for a minute to consider when Abraham's faith was strengthened. In the midst of a lingering impossibility. Yet, his faith was not weakened, nor did it waver. Instead, it was strengthened. Has your faith been strengthened or encouraged in an impossible situation? If so, when?

   b. Review Romans 4:23-24. What was imputed to you?

6. a. Through what response was it imputed (ascribed, assigned, credited) to you? v. 24

   b. What is your part? v. 24

   c. In whom have you believed? v. 24

   d. What miracle did He perform to guarantee your resurrection?

Note: Through this prophesied act (review Romans 4:24), the atoning work of salvation was complete.

   e. From Romans 4:25, what was accomplished and complete?

7. As you close today's lesson, you will record Romans 4:21 in the following exercise. It provides the perfect example of what it means to believe in God. It places total confidence in God's ability, integrity, and performance. As His child, never doubt the fulfillment of His promises. Although we are in a hurry and are generally impatient, God always does what He promised in His perfect timing. Abraham was confidently resting in God's ability and willingness to carry out His promise. Abraham helplessly relied wholly on God. Now, that's faith!

Your Response To God's Word.

Are you currently waiting on a promise from God's word? He is faithful to all His promises. If so, you are invited to follow in Abraham's footsteps. Review Romans 4:20-21.

   a. Record Romans 4:21 below.

   b. As you record the verse, pray that your faith be strengthened and encouraged, just like Abraham's. Reckon it so! God is able and willing to accomplish all that He has promised.

   c. Give glory to God.

d. Rest and hope in God. He is faithful who has promised.

Words From Jesus
"If you abide in Me, and My words abide in you, ask whatever you wish, and it will be done for you" (John 15:7).

Lesson 6: Destiny: Death Through Adam vs. Life Through Christ
Romans 5

Day One: **Read**. Prayerfully read Romans 5.

Memory Verse: "Therefore, having been justified by faith, we have peace with God through our Lord Jesus Christ" (Romans 5:1).

This week's memory verse summarizes Paul's inspired message from Romans chapters 1 - 4. Romans 5 highlights the results of faith. Please review Romans 5:1-5 and answer the following questions:

1. How are you justified?

2. As a result of justification, you have what? _____ _____

3. Through whom? _____

4. Review Romans 5:1-2. In light of your new standing, you experience two fruits of your justification. What are they?

   a. "we have" (you have) v. 1

   b. "we have" (you have) v. 2

5. Romans 5:3-5 addresses the suffering and tribulation of the saints. It's not heaven until heaven. We will know heartache and sorrow in this life—things like illness, death, even persecution will occur. James 1:2-4 echoes Paul's thoughts on tribulation. Both agree that affliction tests faith, and that's a good thing.

   a. Complete the following phrases from Romans 5:3-5.

"And not only *that*, but we also _____ in _____, knowing that _____ produces _____; and perseverance, _____; and character, _____."

   b. Notice the word *glory* in the first phrase of verse 3. It means to *boast or rejoice*. When, if ever, have you boast or rejoiced during one of life's trying times?

6. Review Romans 5:5 and answer the following questions:

Hope does not_____

What was received?_____

Where was it received?_____

How was it received?_____

7. Although our trials produce spiritual benefits like perseverance, sometimes translated as patience, they are not easy to endure. Thinking biblically, what does it mean to have patience? How is this a good thing? How is it evidenced in your life?

8. Jesus knew that you would endure hardships and tribulations. Read John 16:33 and record His promise.

9. Prayerfully read and complete James 1:3-4.

"Knowing that the_____ of your_____ produces patience. But let _____ have *its* perfect _____, that you may be _____ and _____, lacking nothing."

You are not delivered from your trials and tribulations but rather in and through them. You grow and mature because of them. Your confidence and hope in Jesus are enriched when you are facing persecution and difficulties. All believers are tested! Abraham was facing a promised child's dilemma accompanied by the reality of many, many years of a loving marriage that produced no offspring. You will recall from last week's lesson, his faith and hope remained unwavering. (See Romans 4:20.) Paul was also tested repeatedly. According to his testimony, he confessed that he'd been thrice shipwrecked, beaten, left for dead, lost at sea, etc. Many troubles beset him. (See 2

Corinthians 11:25-27.) His faith was increased, and sin did not burn within him as a result of these tribulations. Have you not been tested?

As you conclude today's lesson, prayerfully reflect on your most recent trial. Were your prayers not more passionate, more frequent, and more honest as a result of your suffering? As you faced this trial, was Christ's loving embrace not more precious and near? Like Abraham and Paul, the truth of scripture must guide your life, not emotions or circumstances. Get alone with Jesus today and spend some time glorifying your Father in heaven. Rejoice! Enter His courts with praise and thanksgiving! He has saved you, and His keeping faith affords you heightened spiritual growth through every passing trial. You are invited to pray.

Lesson 6: Destiny: Death Through Adam vs. Life Through Christ
Romans 5

Day Two: **Research**. Review Romans 5.

Memory Verse: "Therefore, having been justified by faith, we have peace with God through our Lord Jesus Christ" (Romans 5:1).

Using a bible, bible dictionary, or concordance define the following *keywords*.

a. *tribulation* v. 3

b. *perseverance* vv. 3; 4

c. *hope* vv. 4; 5

d. ***offense*** vv. 15; 16; 18; 20

e. ***grace*** vv. 2; 15; 20; 21

II. Read the following **key phrases**.

peace with God v. 1- In the NT, the word "peace" had many uses. It was used as an oral or written greeting or farewell. It also referenced a state of being or a state of mind like tranquility. Its NT usage was also extended to describe the opposite of "disorder or persecution." In this particular sense, however, it describes more than a state of mind, or an inward and outward peace, and much more than a relational disposition among men. It also referenced more than salvation. From this passage, *"peace"* referenced man's standing. That peace represented their status or position before God, and it was linked to the judgment of God. "Peace" in this sense implies that man is at peace with God as opposed to being at war with God. Sin separated humanity from God, beginning in the garden. That means we were all enemies of God. (See Romans 5:10.) The peace of Romans 5:1 expresses the polar opposite; we are no longer enemies of God. We are at peace with our Creator. We have been "justified by faith" because we have believed. Read Romans 5:1 and Romans 8:6.

access by faith v. 2 - Referencing the Greek-English Lexicon of the NT, we find through the word's root meaning, *"the right or opportunity to address someone, implying the higher status of the person addressed—'approach, access.' "* All believers enjoy access to the throne of grace. The veil was rent from top to bottom when Jesus died on the cross. Therefore, you can enter boldly into His presence because He has provided you access.

From Ephesians 3:12 - What do we have and through whom?

From Hebrews 4:16 – What will we obtain and what will we find?

saved from wrath v. 9 - saved - ***sōzō*** in Greek meaning *to save, deliver; keep.* A review of the anatomy of the original verb in this passage reveals something quite beautiful - surety! Paul uses a particular verb tense, voice, and mood to expand the verb's primary meaning. From the original text, the verb appears in the future tense, has a passive voice, and is in the indicative mood. What does that tell you? Simply this: the ultimate satisfaction or fulfillment of salvation will occur in the future. Paul uses the term "save" to cover more than the reality or state of salvation in this present life. For clarity, let's spotlight the verb usage. The passive voice means the subject (the sinner) is the recipient of the verbal action (salvation) presently (as in declared and experientially) and in the life to come (this addresses the end times reality and fulfillment). Therefore, we can conclude that Paul's inspired words note your present position or standing before God, accompanied by the surety of futuristic fulfillment. As a believer, you are spared, saved, delivered, and kept from God's wrath. God's wrath is the punishment that was due you as a penalty for your sins. God's Word assures you of your salvation and deliverance from sin. That means deliverance presently, as well as from sins' eternal consequences.

From Romans 10:9 – What must you do? What will you gain?

From Romans 10:17 – How does faith come?

having been reconciled v. 10 - From *The Greek-English Lexicon of the NT reconciled* means *"to reestablish proper friendly interpersonal relations after these have been disrupted or broken."* Through Adam, sin in the garden separated humanity from God - that includes you. Unless we are restored or reconciled, we will remain separated from God. Reconciliation is a spiritual transaction. It restores you to the authentic or original relationship that God desired and intended. Remember, God created you for fellowship with Him; you exist at God's divine pleasure. The reconciliation transaction comes from God, and it only occurs when you come to saving faith.

Record 1 Corinthians 1:9 below and underline the first three words of the verse.

one man's disobedience v. 19 - refers to Adam's trespass, offense, or sin through which all humanity is declared guilty. One theologian stated, *"Because all humanity existed in the loins of Adam, and have through procreation inherited his "fallenness" and depravity, it can be said that all sinned in him."* As a result of Adam's sin - sin entered humanity. It became part of our nature. In other words, Adam passed the intrinsic or natural disposition to sin to all his descendants through his first disobedience. King David lamented over his sinful disposition, realizing man's sinful nature is present from the moment of conception. He declared we were born in sin because we were conceived in sin. He understood without God's intervention that sin made it impossible for man to live a life that was pleasing to God.

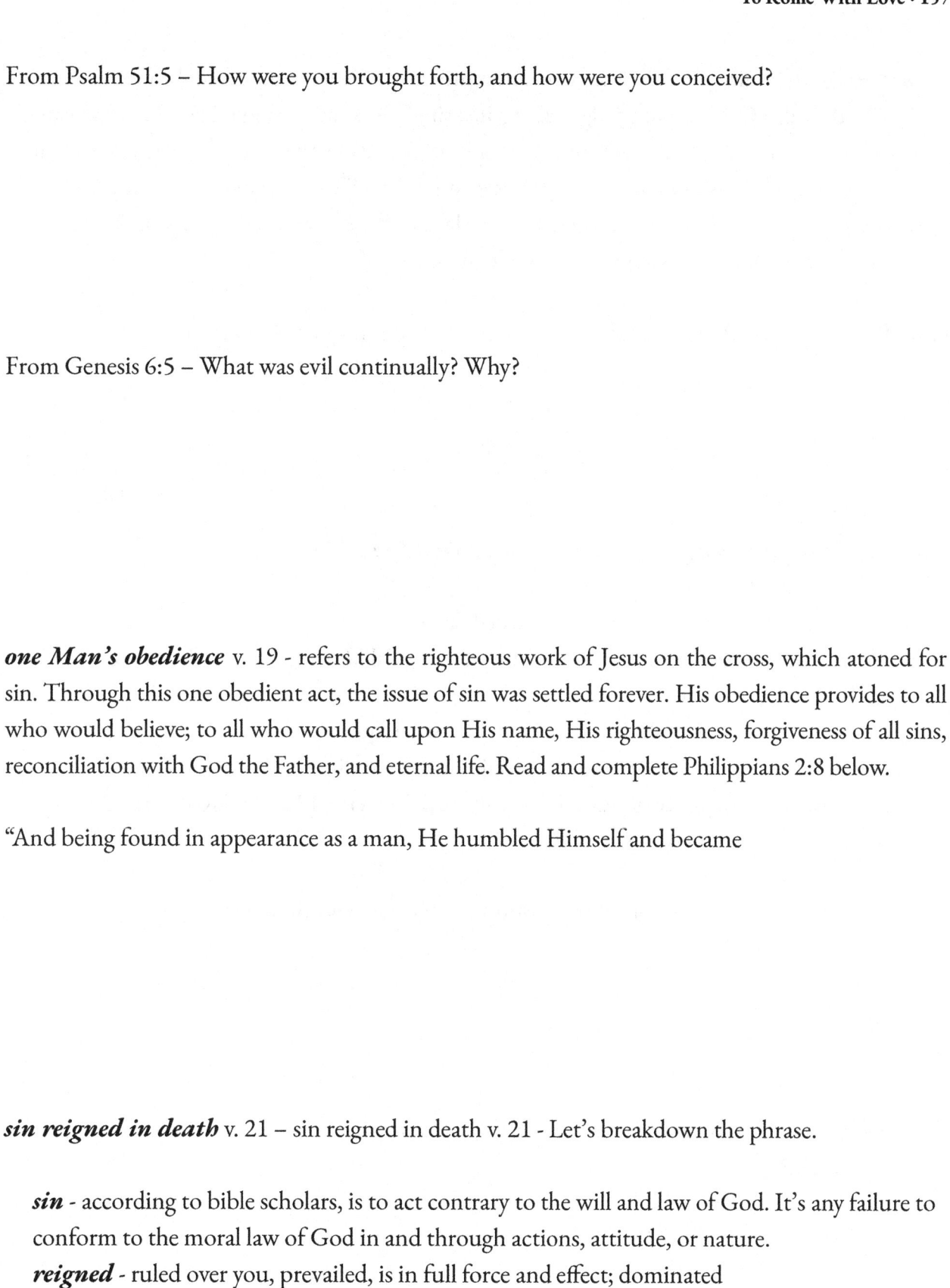

From Psalm 51:5 – How were you brought forth, and how were you conceived?

From Genesis 6:5 – What was evil continually? Why?

one Man's obedience v. 19 - refers to the righteous work of Jesus on the cross, which atoned for sin. Through this one obedient act, the issue of sin was settled forever. His obedience provides to all who would believe; to all who would call upon His name, His righteousness, forgiveness of all sins, reconciliation with God the Father, and eternal life. Read and complete Philippians 2:8 below.

"And being found in appearance as a man, He humbled Himself and became

sin reigned in death v. 21 – sin reigned in death v. 21 - Let's breakdown the phrase.

>***sin*** - according to bible scholars, is to act contrary to the will and law of God. It's any failure to conform to the moral law of God in and through actions, attitude, or nature.
>***reigned*** - ruled over you, prevailed, is in full force and effect; dominated

in death - sin results in death; leads to death; unto death. Death is the natural consequence of sin. Death is also God's express judgment against sin. When sin entered the world, death came as well. Death is trifold. There is a spiritual death or separation from God, a physical death, and eternal death, which is sometimes called the second death. This death not only includes eternal separation from God but eternal torment in the lake of fire as well. (See Revelation 20:14-15.) Read Romans 6:23 and answer the following question.

From Romans 6:23 – What is death and, in contrast, what is the gift of God?

grace might reign through righteousness to eternal life v. 21.

grace - literally God's unmerited and unearned favor
might reign – literally will rule over you, prevail, is in full force and effect; dominate
though - by the means of
righteousness – literally right living; doing what God requires; doing what is right
to eternal life - literally everlasting life; pertaining to an unlimited duration of time; life without end in the presence of Jesus. For clarity, read Proverbs 12:28 and Romans 6:22 and answer the following questions.

From Proverbs 12:28 – In the way of righteousness is life, what is not in its pathway?

From Romans 6:22 – Now that we have been set free from sin, becoming slaves to God, what fruit is promised?

Lesson 6: Destiny: Death Through Adam vs. Life Through Christ
Romans 5

Day Three: **Receive.** Prayerfully read Romans 5.

Memory Verse: "Therefore, having been justified by faith, we have peace with God through our Lord Jesus Christ" (Romans 5:1).

Review Romans 5:6-11 and answer the following questions.

1. Review Romans 5:6. What happened when you were without strength?

2. Read Romans 5:7. What might one scarcely consider for a righteous man or a good man?

3. Read Romans 5:8. In your own words, explain what Christ accomplished.

4. What were the results? Read Romans 5:9 and complete the following:

Much more then, having now been _____ by _____
_____, we shall be _____ from _____ through Him.

5. You are hidden with Christ in God. You are His; you are safe in the beloved! What does this mean to you? You are invited to share.

6. Review Romans 5:10. You are saved by what? Be specific.

7. Romans 5:11 says much more than that. Your heart responded because it received something unique and amazing!

   a. What was your heart's response through our Lord Jesus Christ?

b. What was accomplished that causes you immense gladness and joy through our Lord Jesus Christ?

8. Romans 5:11 clearly states that you received reconciliation. Everything the Lord does has eternal purpose and benefit. Thinking biblically, what are the benefits of reconciliation? In the space below, you are invited to share scripture to define the benefits.

9. Believers are reconciled, and according to 2 Corinthians 5:18, you have received a ministry that accompanies it. What was it? Read and record 2 Corinthians 5:18 below to discover your answer. Underline the last word.

2 Corinthians 5:18

10. Thinking biblically, what is the ministry of reconciliation, and what does it invite you to do?

♥ Heart-Check For Today.

You conclude today's lesson by receiving God's Word into your heart. Prayerfully consider the benefits of reconciliation in your own life. Give thanks and glory to God! You have been reconciled to Him through Jesus Christ! Consequently, who might you need to be reconciled with presently? That's between you and God; however, you are invited to consider God's overall reconciliation plan as you complete questions 11 and 12.

11. God has given you the ministry of reconciliation. He is faithful to reconcile you to Himself as well as believers one to another. Remember the powerful words of Jesus, "all will know you by your love." John 13:35. As Jesus was announcing His departure to His disciples, He spoke passionately about love. Not only His enduring and faithful love for them but their love for others. In verse 34, He issued a new commandment. What was it? Read and complete John 13:34 below. It echoes the greatest commandment of Mark 12:28-31.

"A new _____ I give to you, that you _____ one another; as I have _____ _____, that you also _____ _____ another" (John 13:34).

12. With God's love for you in mind, would you commit to pray for reconciliation where it is needed? It may appear hopeless, but God is faithful in this ministry. His love will prevail; it reconciled you! God's love covers a multitude of sins. Did it not cover yours? No matter how great the offender's wrong, even an offense against you, it was handled on Calvary. Christ has paid for that same offense in full! Remember too.

According to Solomon, a gentle word turns away wrath.

"A soft answer turns away wrath, but a harsh word stirs up anger" (Proverbs 15:1).

In the words of the famous Bulgarian proverb: "A gentle word opens an iron gate." Rejoice! Even an iron gate cannot impede the love of God and His ministry of reconciliation. You are invited to stop and pray for reconciliation now. These prayers delight God's heart!

Lesson 6: Destiny: Death Through Adam vs. Life Through Christ
Romans 5

Day Four: **Reflect.** Prayerfully review Romans 5.

Memory Verse: "Therefore, having been justified by faith, we have peace with God through our Lord Jesus Christ" (Romans 5:1).

Read Romans 5:12-16 and answer questions 1-7.

1. Paul draws a conclusion in Romans 5:12. According to Paul, what entered the world through one man, and how was it spread?

2. Review Romans 5:12, who was the one man?

3. Thinking biblically, explain how "all sinned."

4. From Romans 5:13, what was not imputed when there was no law?

5. Review Romans 5:14. Nevertheless, what reigned and why?

6. There was a free gift, not like the offense. Read Romans 5:15. What was "the gift by the grace of the one Man, Jesus Christ..." ?

7. Read Romans 5:16 and answer the following questions. Where possible, record the exact words of the verse.

   a. This gift is different. How so?_____

   b. Judgment resulted in what?_____

   c. Define *condemnation*.

   d. Where does justification come in?_____

Read Romans 5:17 and answer questions 8-10.

8. Complete Romans 5:17 to discover the two amazing things that will reign in your life through the One, Jesus Christ.

"For if by the one man's offense death reigned through the one, much more those who receive _____ _____ _____ and of the_____ _____ _____ will reign in _____ through the One, Jesus Christ" (Romans 5:17).

9. From the first phrase of verse 17, we see through Adam's sin that the entire human race was subject to death. In the words that follow, Paul draws a stark contrast to the vast effects and benefits of Christ's single act of obedience. Paul states, "much more" the benefits. Some translations read "how much more, or it is far greater." The implication is its effects and benefits are too vast to imagine, and mere words don't do it justice! Paul implies much more the benefits, far more significant the outcome, in this present life and in the life to come. Paul spotlights Christ's act as far more meaningful for all humans than what Satan had planned. God trumps evil. He always wins! One bible scholar summarized this verse by stating, "God's grace is infinitely greater for good than Adam's sin is for evil." The enemy had a plan, but God had the best plan! His work is not merely good or better, it's always best, and He always accomplishes His desired purpose. As a sweet reminder, record John 3:16 below.

10. Look at the last phrase of Romans 5:17, "...will reign in life through the One, Jesus Christ." Christ died so that you could have eternal life, as well as an abundant spiritual life today. So the question for discussion is this. "Are you *in 'Adam* or *in Christ*?*'* If you are *in Adam*, sin and death reign over your life, and you live under condemnation. But, if you are *in Christ,* grace reigns over your life through Christ. As a result, sin no longer has you bound. In Christ, you are no longer a slave to sin. For clarity, let's break it down.

Adam's act of rebellion led to death, naturally, spiritually, and eternally, but Christ's atoning act brought life. Not just life, but abundant life, abundant grace, and righteousness! From *The Greek-*

English Lexicon of the NT reign means *"to be in control in an absolute manner—'to reign, to control completely.'"* Therefore, from our verse, Christ's death brought life and abundant grace and righteousness. To what? To reign and control your life - entirely - through Jesus Christ.

From verse 17, notice the words, *will reign.* That's a done deal, not a maybe. Jesus' death will accomplish all that He intended. So you might wonder, what does that look like in my life? Not to oversimplify, but It looks like Christ. As His spirit rules and reigns in us, we look like Jesus! What's that? It's a confident, purposeful life that honors God and celebrates peace with Him and with your fellow man as much as possible. (See Romans 12:18.) That life – a life with Christ's Spirit reigning, bears good fruit, and has eternity in view. Its words, actions, thoughts, and deeds are loving. It is never self-seeking or self-serving. It is always humble. It considers the needs and concerns of others more significant than its own. Lastly, it hates sin and is deeply grieved when it sins.

Do these characteristics reign in you? If not, don't despair. God is faithful, and Jesus' obedient work on Calvary was sufficient and complete. You have all you need. He has left nothing unfinished. He will establish an abundant, productive spiritual life in you (and through you). It's promised! As you abide in Him, walk with Him, and yield to Him daily. As you yield, by dying to self, His Holy Spirit will seal His Word in your heart and bring it to performance in your life. Christ's Spirit **will reign** in you! That's what Paul said. Record one of God's most precious promises below. With each word, notice who is doing the work!

Philippians 1:6

11. In Romans 5:18-19, Paul summarizes the analogy between Adam and Christ. Read the verses and complete the following.

"Therefore, as through _____ man's offense _____ came to _____ men, resulting in _____, even so through one Man's

_____ act *the*_____ _____ *came* to _____
_____, resulting in _____ of life. 19 For as by one man's _____ _____ were made _____, so also by one Man's _____ many will be made _____."

12. Rejoice! You are a righteous saint! You didn't earn it, and you couldn't buy it. Give thanks and glory to God. Through one Man's obedience – **Jesus Christ** - you were made righteous. Only God could accomplish this! You will have the opportunity to respond in tomorrow's lesson. For today, look back to the theme verse of Romans. Prayerfully review Romans 1:16-17 to remember how "the redeemed shall live." Record verse 17 below.

Romans 1:17

Lesson 6: Destiny: Death Through Adam vs. Life Through Christ
Romans 5

Day Five: **Respond.** Prayerfully review Romans 5.

Weekly Memory Verse: "Therefore, having been justified by faith, we have peace with God through our Lord Jesus Christ" (Romans 5:1).

1. We kick off today's lesson with an overview of Paul's inspired message of Romans 5. In verses 6-11, Paul teaches about substitutionary atonement. That means Christ took your sin upon Himself and died for you on the cross. In Romans 5:12-21, he teaches about your identification. You are hidden with Christ in God. When God looks at you, He sees Jesus, and because you have believed in Him, His righteousness is yours! Now, by grace, you can live an abundant life and enjoy victory over sin. Paul sums it all up in the last two verses. Review Romans 5:20-21 and complete the passage below.

"Moreover the _____ entered that the _____ might abound. But where _____ abounded, _____ abounded much more, so that as sin _____ in death, even so _____ might _____ through _____ to eternal life through _____ _____ our Lord" (Romans 5:20-21).

Paul uses many contrasts in Romans 5. The overarching difference is Adam and Christ. Read and review the chart below, which summarizes Romans 5:15-21.

<u>Verses</u>	<u>Contrast</u>	<u>Explanation</u>
15-16	**Offense vs God's free gift**	Adam's offense brought condemnation and death *vs.* God's free gift, which brings justification and life.
17	**Death vs Life**	All men were subject to death through Adam *vs.* believers reign in life, now and eternally through Christ.

18	**Condemnation vs. Justification**	Humanity was condemned through Adam. In sin, Adam hid from God *vs.* Through Christ, you have right standing before God; you have access to confess sin and surety of pardon.
19	**Disobedience vs. Obedience**	Through the disobedience of Adam all became sinners *vs.* Through the obedience of Christ, those who believe are made righteous.
20	**Law vs. Grace**	The law revealed sin but could not save *vs.* Grace met and exceeded the demands of the law and provided what the law could never accomplish. Grace provided the only remedy through Christ which is salvation from sin.

2. Paul concludes this powerful message in Romans 5:20-21. You are a new creature in Christ! You have newness of life and salvation! Hope reigns eternal, and it reigns in you! (See Romans 5:17; 21.) Rejoice! You are hidden with Christ in God. Joyfully record 2 Corinthians 5:17 below.

3. The benefits of the abundance of grace and the gift of righteousness are linked to Christ's obedience. Therefore, you cannot conclude this week's study without taking a closer look at obedience and our responsibility towards it. After all, even Christ was obedient. To discover who Christ obeyed, why He was obeyed, and the blessings of obedience, prayerfully read and record the appropriate phrase from each scripture below.

John 6:38 (to whom)

John 4:34 (why)

Romans 5:1 (blessing)

4. What a beautiful conclusion. You have noted throughout this study who had the plan, who has done the work, and who will bring it to full performance - God. In Jesus, God has done it all! Being in Christ, sin no longer reigns. Instead, God's abundant grace and righteousness reign. Death has no victory—instead, life reigns, and hope springs eternal. Lastly, we reign in life and death through Christ Jesus, our Lord. He has made you a king and priest by His grace and for His glory. Read and review Revelation 1:5-6 and answer the following:

Who was the faithful witness?

Who was the firstborn from dead?

Who rules over the kings of the earth?

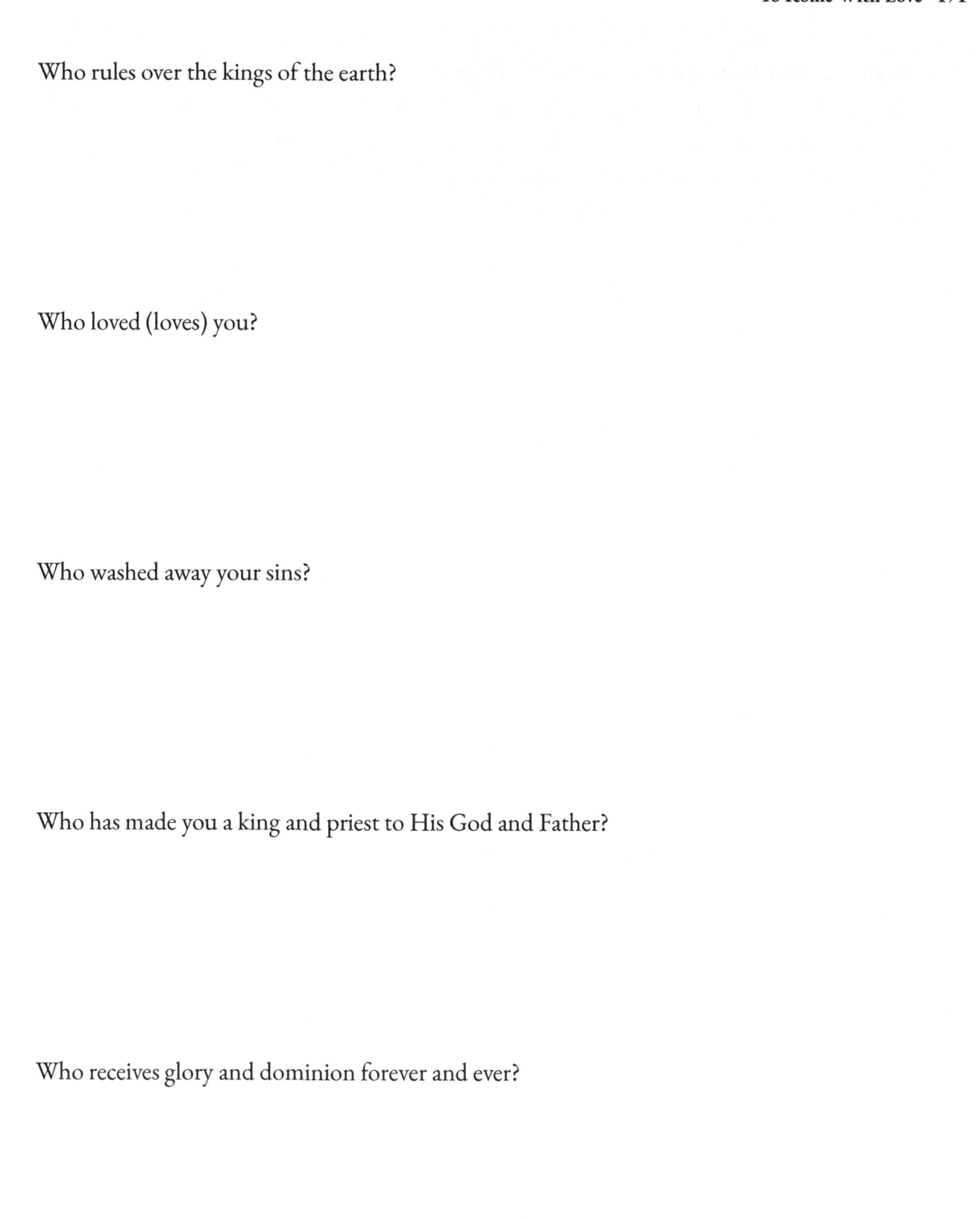

Who loved (loves) you?

Who washed away your sins?

Who has made you a king and priest to His God and Father?

Who receives glory and dominion forever and ever?

5. In closing, is your heart not soaring? He has done all things for you! You have captivated His heart, and He has loved you with an everlasting love from before the foundation of the world. How astounding is that? You are on His heart, on His mind, and in His prayers always. He delights in you! Dear one, you are worth dying for, and it has been accomplished! Prayerfully read and record the beautiful promise of Hebrews 7:25.

Hebrews 7:25

Words From Jesus
"I am the good shepherd. The good shepherd gives His life for the sheep" (John 10:11).

Lesson 7: Dead To Sin And Alive In Christ
Romans 6:1-14

Romans Road Map: The book of Romans is divided into two major sections. The first section identifies the Redeemed of God and what they believe, while the second section governs their behavior. That's significant because their behavior authenticates the power of the gospel at work in those who are hidden with Christ in God. This life-changing gospel or "good news" is the same gospel of which Paul was unashamed. That truth of the gospel has not changed in any measure since Christ died on Calvary. It's the same gospel unto salvation that empowered Peter and 119 other Spirit-filled believers to burst from the upper room at Pentecost. Their united hearts were willing to lose their lives for the benefit of others. With fearless determination, they decided, "whatever comes may come." To a swelling crowd of thousands, Peter preached the Gospel of God with power and passion. Some believe it was his finest hour. What were the results? The church - Christ's bride - was born. Three thousand sinners came to faith that very day.

We don't sin in a vacuum, and we aren't saved in one either. Just as your sin affects those around you, so much more the benefits of your salvation! Others are blessed because you believe. Remember, many who accompanied the Israelites on their mass Exodus from Egypt were not believers, yet they enjoyed the benefits of traveling along with those who were. They were blessed because they were traveling in the company of God's children. Who's traveling with you? Your husband, your children, grandchildren, siblings, parents, neighbors, and friends? Their lives can be immeasurably blessed as Christ shines in and through you! He'd like to shine through you in every situation or circumstance, both good and bad, including your triumphs and trials. That's why understanding God's work of sanctification is so important. Understanding this life-changing work will enhance your journey. Hopefully, it will inspire you to shine for Christ through the good times and the bad.

Therefore, beginning with today's lesson and continuing for the next five weeks, we will study **sanctification**. What is it, and through what means is it manifested in the lives of believers? We will ask and answer questions like 1). Do I play an active role in this work? 2). Do the choices I make have any bearing on my sanctification? 3). How can I effectively live for Christ? And 4). How does sanctification affect my daily life? Here's a brief overview.

Simply stated, **sanctification** is *"a progressive work of God and man that makes us more and more free from sin and more like Christ in our actual lives."*[3] As you can see from Dr. Grudem's definition, we participate in this work by co-laboring with Christ's Spirit, which resides in us. Not only has His righteousness been imputed to all who believe, but His Spirit embodies us the moment we believe. Those results are manifested spiritually and naturally. How so? You not only enjoy the benefits of knowing you're saved and have right standing (justification) before a Holy God, but you can enjoy freedom from sin's grasp as well. Ideally, coming to faith means you are declared right (spiritually) and can live right (naturally)!

An overview of Romans chapters 1- 8:

Romans 1 - 3:20 The *how and why* of salvation and our unrighteousness in light of God's righteousness.

Romans 3:21 - 5 Our justification which is our righteousness imputed.

Romans 6 - 8 Our sanctification which is our righteousness imparted.

Day One: **Read**. Prayerfully read Romans 6:1-14.

Memory Verse: "Therefore we were buried with Him through baptism into death, that just as Christ was raised from the dead by the glory of the Father, even so we also should walk in newness of life" (Romans 6:4).

1. Paul begins chapter 6 with a dialogue concerning sin and grace. He believed those who loved sin would assume a license to sin. How so? When they heard that God's grace was most bountiful in the greatest sins, Paul believed it might cheapen grace and give way to enormous sins.

Let's review what we've recently studied. Read and record Romans 5:20 below.

Romans 5:20 –

---

3   Grudem, W. A. (2004). *Systematic theology: an introduction to biblical doctrine* (p. 1253). Leicester, England; Grand Rapids, MI: Inter-Varsity Press; Zondervan Pub. House.

2. Review Romans 5:20. What entered that the offense might abound?

3. What abounded much more than sin?

Read Romans 6:1-2 and answer the following questions:

4. In Pauline fashion, he asks and answers his posed question. What does Paul ask in Romans 6:1?

5. With a forceful, two-word response, Paul answered in Romans 6:1. What was his reply?

6. What were we not to "live in" any longer?

7. From previous lessons, we have agreed that sin has an end. What is it? Record a verse in support of your answer.

8. Paul declares that *sin is not* an option for those in Christ Jesus. Review Romans 6:2 and record the important words of the second phrase of the verse below.

9. Read Romans 6:3. Into what two things were you baptized?

10. Sin matters to God; it always has. Because it matters to God, it should matter to us! Paul had much to say about sin to the church of Corinth. Prayerfully read 1 Corinthians 6:9-11.

    a. From 1 Corinthians 6:9, What is the one word classification that Paul uses to identify those who will not inherit the kingdom of God? _____

    b. In 1 Corinthians 6:9-10, Paul issues a sharp warning. Complete the verses below. "Do you not know that the unrighteous will not inherit the kingdom of God? Do not be _____. Neither fornicators, nor idolaters, nor adulterers, nor homosexuals, nor sodomites, nor thieves, nor covetous, nor drunkards, nor revilers, nor executioners will inherit the kingdom of God."

11. According to Paul, some will not inherit the kingdom. In 1 Corinthians 6: 9–10, Paul lists ten unrepentant sins or lifestyles that will keep people out of God's kingdom. Please list them below:

1._____

2._____

3._____

4._____

5._____

6._____

7._____

8._____

9._____

10._____

Prayerfully review the list. *These* will not inherit the kingdom, nor are *they* included in God's spiritual kingdom presently. Paul's words identify unrepentant behavior and lifestyles, not the occasional sins of believers, which we quickly repent. Thankfully, with confession and repentance, we are immediately restored. As believers, we have the promise of pardon and the surety of reconciliation.

In 1 Corinthians 6:9-10, Paul references a lifestyle of sin. That would be unconfessed and unrepentant habitual sins, which not only reveal the absence of God's Spirit but the lack of salvation as well. Remember, the moment you come to faith, you are given the Holy Spirit. He is not withheld. Instead, He is a deposit and your guarantee of life with Christ forever. His Spirit seals your heart and brings God's word to performance in your life. When He resides in you, you become a new creature who lives to holiness, not perversion and sin. The old sin man has died, and Christ's Spirit resides and reigns in you.

Rejoice! You belong to Jesus now and forever. Bible scholars agree that while believers sometimes commit these sins, they do not adopt them as a lifestyle. People of great faith obey God and delight in His Word. One theologian said it like this, "When they do [long for perversion and sin], it demonstrates that the person is not in God's kingdom. True believers who do sin resent that sin and seek to gain the victory over it." In the coming weeks, we will examine this Christian principle as we study Romans 7:14-25.

12. Complete the words of 1 Corinthians 6:11.

"And such _____ some of you. But you were _____, but you were _____, but you were _____ in the name of the Lord _____ and by the _____ of our God."

13. Read Romans 6:4 and answer the following:

   a. How were we buried with Him? Be specific.

b. What occurred by the glory of the Father?

c. What was Paul's summary in Romans 6:4? Complete the last phrase below.

"...even so,

_____."

14. Thinking biblically, what does it mean to walk in newness of life? Are you walking in newness of life?

Lesson 7: Dead To Sin And Alive In Christ
Romans 6:1-14

Day Two: **Research**. Prayerfully review Romans 6:1-14.

Memory Verse: "Therefore we were buried with Him through baptism into death, that just as Christ was raised from the dead by the glory of the Father, even so we also should walk in newness of life" (Romans 6:4).

II. Using a bible, bible dictionary, or concordance, define the following *keywords*.

grace v. 1, 14

abound v. 1

baptized; baptism v. 3, 4

reckon v. 11

dominion v. 9, 14

II. Read the following **key phrases.**

died to sin v. 2, 10 – Is the fundamental premise of Romans 6. *According to the Greek-English Lexicon of the NT, this is a figurative extension of the meaning "to die." It means "to be unable to respond or react to any impulse or desire—'to be dead to, to not respond to, to have no part in.' Also, to cease, to stop; having stopped sinning or ceased sinning. To be like dead as far as desiring to sin' or 'to be like a corpse as far as temptations to sin are concerned.' "* We can agree that dying to sin is not obeying the cravings of sin or succumbing to its will. We are in Christ. As believers, we participate in Christ's death and resurrection. Christ's death to sin becomes our death to sin, so we are dead to sin. Therefore, how can a "dead one" sin? Peter echoes this premise when he suggests that you must live to righteousness as a result of Christ's work on Calvary (on your behalf). At its base meaning, it's *knowing the right thing and doing it, turning from sin, and with a thankful heart living to glorify God.* Prayerfully read 1 Peter 2:24.

baptized into Christ Jesus v. 3 - This is not water baptism. Paul was speaking in a metaphorical sense. It references a spiritual baptism that puts us into Christ. At the moment of salvation, we are given His Holy Spirit, and we become members of His body. We are in Christ; we are hidden with Christ in God. That identifies a spiritual immersion that unites and connects us with Him. For clarity, in most cases, water baptism soon follows. It is an outward testimony of this inward spiritual change - an immersion, transaction, and manifestation of Christ IN YOU. It signifies that you belong to Jesus, inside and out! It is also an act of scriptural obedience. (See Acts 2:38.) Baptism confirms that you know, trust, and understand that Christ died not only for humanity's sins but for yours too. It's personal! You have repented and received Christ's pardon. Moving forward, you are hidden with Christ in God; baptized into Christ Jesus; reckon yourself dead to sin, and yield to His Spirit who reigns within you.

From 1 Corinthians 6:17 – What happens when you are joined to the Lord?

baptized into His death v. 3 - That spiritual immersion or identification is linked explicitly to Christ's death and resurrection. Upon coming to faith, all believers are united to Christ and identified with Christ. Note: Romans 6:4-7 records the best explanation of this baptism.

Galatians 3:27 (Note: This verse is the essential reference to the Christian ordinance of baptism in all of Paul's writings.) Record the verse below.

newness of life v. 4 - From *The Greek-English Lexicon of the NT* – *"the state of being new and different, with the implication of superiority—'newness.'"* That speaks of regeneration, which comes from the Latin word *regenerare* meaning *create again*. You are a new creature. The old creature has passed away, it has died, and it has been buried. Something dead has absolutely no life and cannot respond to anything. With the newness of life, you have a new point of reference. What is it? It's Christ IN YOU! Your life has new, purposeful, and unique qualities, which hold and shape your character, nature, and direction. Worldly, trivial things that once seemed important now have no place or meaning in your life. New principles for life now govern you - you honor God and yield to God. You inquire of God. In short, you are guided by God's Word and delight to fulfill His will and purposes. You have reckoned yourself dead to sin - all sin. You have been raised in the newness of life, having put on the righteousness of Christ and live accordingly. Read 2 Corinthians 5:17 and Ephesians 4:22-24.

Out with the old and in with the new! Life has new a meaning and purpose. Subsequently, many things you once held dear have no meaning or purpose in your life. What former things have your new life caused you to dismiss as useless, unimportant, or insignificant, which you once held dear? What worldly pursuits and pleasure have you "let go" as a new creature in Christ?

crucified with Him v. 6 - Your old nature, character, and point of reference, "self and sin," died with Jesus. Sin always has the same destiny. After exhausting itself to its end, it's always death. The good news is that only death can open the door for resurrection. Without death, there is no resurrection. One scholar noted, "death had a definite purpose in the spiritual life and history of the believer." We were crucified so that our sinful nature be rendered powerless. The Greek verb **katargeō** means *being reduced to a condition of absolute impotence and inaction - as if it were dead.* Once dead and powerless, sin has no hold over you. In Christ, you were set free from the bondage of sin. From this point forward, sin is powerless to dominate or control your new life. Prayerfully read Paul's testimony of Galatians 2:20 and complete the passage. As you record Paul's words, make it personal. After all, you're dead to sin as well! Rejoice! sin has no hold over you.

"_____have been _____ with _____; it is no longer _____who live, but Christ lives in _____; and the _____ which I now live in the flesh I _____ by _____ in the Son of God, who _____ _____ and gave _____ for _____."

reckon yourself dead indeed to sin v. 11 – literally consider, reckon, regard, suppose, you died to your old sin nature - it's pleasures, pursuits, and desires. Christ died once and for all, and although sinless, He took humanity's sin upon Himself; Christ became sin. (See 2 Corinthians 5:21.) Through His death, His relationship with all sin was ended. It ended yours too!

Consequently, you are no longer living under sin's dominion or control. In this verse, the verbal action in the original language is gripping. Let's take a closer look.

First, "reckon" appears in the imperative mood; therefore, it is a command. In Romans 6:11, Paul calls upon our faith. That means, by faith, you must reckon yourself dead to sin; consider yourself dead to sin; because of Christ's finished work on Calvary. As you can see, our faith participates in the "reckoning." Apart from faith, reckoning never occurs.

Second, "reckon" appears in the middle or passive voice. The verb translated "count or reckon" ***logizomai*** is being affected by its action or is acting upon itself. That's where the faith comes in. *The Theological Dictionary of the New Testament* states, "Thus, the obedient apprehension of the reality of faith poses the demand that life should be subordinated to this reality." We must agree with God – we are dead to sin. It further concludes, "The imperative (command or intention) of Romans 6:11 implies that the believer's conduct should be in conformity with this judgment of faith." In essence, "you've believed, now behave accordingly." Let your life confirm your confession of faith.

From the original language, it's clearly seen that Paul links Christ's work on the cross to our judgment of faith. Do you believe Christ's death sufficiently handled your sin(s) or not? This "counting or reckoning" must be oriented to the facts established by the reality of God. God has declared this work sufficient. It was enough to handle all sin, forever. That's why the verbal action of this verse becomes a "judgment of faith." It calls for our faith to rise (up) in response! What are the results, naturally and spiritually?

Since Christ lives and reigns in unbroken fellowship with God and since you are "in Christ" (your relationship with sin h ended), you, too, can live in unbroken fellowship and harmony with your Heavenly Father. That's the coveted goal for believers. (Is it not?) Celebrating and enjoying unbroken fellowship with God in Christ Jesus! Regardless of your past, all who God has justified will experience personal holiness. We must remember; however, **unrepentant sin always separates us from God.** Read Colossians 3:3.

Who died, and what were the results? For your response, record the verse below.

Colossians 3:3 -

alive to God in Christ Jesus v. 11 - Through Christ's death and resurrection, we are alive to God in Christ. You live and have your being by God's grace and for His glory. Your purpose for life has changed, and you have a new direction. You have turned from sin. If you are alive to God in Christ Jesus, you must be dead to sin. There is no other formula. Read and complete Ephesians 2:4-5 below.

"But _____, who is _____ in _____, because of His great _____ with which He loved _____, **5** even when we were _____ in trespasses, made us _____ together with _____ (by _____ you have been _____)..." (Ephesians 2:4-5).

Lesson 7: Dead To Sin And Alive In Christ
Romans 6:1-14

Day Three: **Receive**. Review Romans 6:1-14.

Memory Verse: "Therefore we were buried with Him through baptism into death, that just as Christ was raised from the dead by the glory of the Father, even so we also should walk in newness of life" (Romans 6:4).

1. From Romans 6:5, Paul declares if you are united with Christ in one way, you are most certainly connected with him in another. According to Paul, through what two methods (means) are we united to Christ?

2. As Paul continues to build his argument against a life dominated by sin, he makes three "that" statements in Romans 6:6. What are they?

   1. knowing **that**_____

   2. **that** the body_____

   3. **that** we_____

3. Read Romans 6:7. What was the glorious outcome? Record the verse below.

Romans 6:7

4. Pastor and theologian R.C. Sproul noted this concerning Romans 6:7. "We have experienced the greatest exodus that is possible for human beings: we have been freed from sin." Reread Romans 6:7 and record the first thoughts that come to mind as you reckon yourself free/freed from sin. You are invited to share.

When you know the truth, you can reckon it so in your own life and respond to Christ by yielding to His Holy Spirit. You can rejoice. All things appear settled. You are freed from sin – past, present, and future! But, just when you think sin is ended, you find yourself sinning – again! That's because we are spirit and flesh, and all believers wrestle with sin - some more than others. Even Paul wrestled with sin. Only Jesus lived an earthly life that was free of sin. Paul will address this topic in Romans 7. The truth of the matter is this. Believers still live in bodies made of flesh; therefore, sin will be an ongoing reality until Christ calls us home. Remember, too. We live in a fallen world that belongs to Satan. He holds many captive to sin - sin is all around us – it's everywhere. Two important things need to be said on the matter.

First, In Romans 6:1-7, Paul outlined the spiritual reality of Christ's work on Calvary and what that means in the life of believers. He gives a detailed account of the spiritual transaction that occurs through Christ's death concerning sin.

Second, although the word clearly states that we are freed from sin, the war within us rages on as our old sinful nature still has some residual effects in our life. Nonetheless, through it all, Paul assures us that "not sinning" is an option. It's a better choice and delights the heart of God. Recently deceased Pastor Kim Clement suggested that God sees you " somewhere in the future, and you look much better than you do right now!"

We owe our thanks to God. His work is sufficient, it was enough, and when He looks at believers, thankfully, He sees Jesus! He sees what He has destined you to become through the death of His beloved Son; He sees the finished work of Jesus' death concerning you! "It is finished," and He sees that spiritual work accomplished. He sees the reality of who you are, even though you feel frail, frazzled, and sometimes fearful. Rejoice – it is accomplished, achieved, and complete! Now, reckon it so! Joyfully live it and walk in it, looking to Him, the perfecter of our faith. He will not only see you through, but He will carry you through. He has promised that He will never leave you or forsake you. (See Hebrews 13:5 and Deuteronomy 31:6.)

5. You have reason to rejoice! Write a brief prayer of thanksgiving below.

6. Read Romans 6:8-9 and answer the following questions. Where possible, record words from the passage in your response.

   1. In verse 8, Paul supposes something in the first phrase. What is it?

   2. Where would we live as a result?

   3. In Romans 6:9, what would we know about Christ?

4. And, what are the results relative to death?

7. What was accomplished in Romans 6:10? Record the verse below.

8. For clarity and reinforcement, in Romans 6:10, _____ died to _____; but He lives to _____.

9. Read Romans 6:11. What does it mean to be dead to sin? Make it personal. You are invited to share a testimony concerning your walk in newness of life.

10. Prayerfully reflect over today's verses – Romans 6:1-11. Jesus' death on Calvary met the legal requirements to satisfy the wrath of God. Review each verse and record the words which best highlight Christ's work of atonement on your behalf.

Romans 6:10

John 1:29

Jesus rendered sin powerless over those who believe in Him. In Christ, we have reconciliation and are alive to God. Peter sums up the great doctrine of substitutionary atonement which is the heart of the gospel by saying: *"who Himself [Jesus] bore our sins in His own body on the tree, that we, having died to sins, might live for righteousness—by whose stripes you were healed" (1 Peter 2:24).*

Conclude today's lesson by receiving God's word into your heart. Jesus' sacrifice was sufficient; it was enough! Moreover, it has liberated you from the grips of sin! Rejoice, it is accomplished, and you are His because you have believed.

You are invited to close in prayer.

Lesson 7: Dead To Sin And Alive In Christ
Romans 6:1-14

Day Four: **Reflect**. Prayerfully read Romans 6:1-14.

Memory Verse: "Therefore we were buried with Him through baptism into death, that just as Christ was raised from the dead by the glory of the Father, even so we also should walk in newness of life" (Romans 6:4).

Romans 6 contains foundational doctrine because it highlights the doctrine of justification by faith. Not to oversimplify the spiritual implications, but justification by faith means we have "right standing" before God because we have believed in Jesus! Reread those words! You are declared not guilty of all sin – past, present, and future because you have believed in Jesus. It's a spiritual transaction that impacts every facet of your life.

The passages before us need closer examination because they reinforce a central theme of Paul's New Testament teaching, which is *death to sin*. The books of Romans, Colossians, and Peter's 1st Epistle confirm and teach that when Christ died, becoming our sin, we died to sin as well. When He was resurrected, we were too - into "newness of life." The text does not say that sin dies to the believer; instead, it is the believer who has died to sin. Until the mountains melt like wax, however, sin and evil within us will remain.

This week's passages reinforce what God has accomplished through Jesus on your behalf. These passages affirm that your baptism into Christ baptized you into Christ's death as well. Christ's **death for sin** becomes your **death to sin**. Noted theologian R. H. Mounce has stated, "The cross was sin's final move; the resurrection was God's checkmate. The game is over. Sin is forever in defeat. Christ the victor died to sin 'once for all' and lives now in unbroken fellowship with God."[4] Having been raised from the dead, Christ can only die once for all. His resurrection has broken the tyranny of death. Paul said that death has "no sting." (See 1 Corinthians 15:55.) Jesus' resurrection not only ended the consequences of sin - it is your guarantee. You will be resurrected with Him! He lives in you – now - and one day, you will be in His presence.

The questions in today's lesson provide time to pause and reflect on the doctrine of justification by faith and how it impacts your life today. Prayerfully answer the following.

---

[4] Mounce, R. H. (1995). *Romans* (Vol. 27, p. 152). Nashville: Broadman & Holman Publishers.

1. What is the first word of Romans 6:12? _____

Paul is drawing a conclusion. He is writing a summary in light of Romans 6:1-11. These verses provide the best scriptural explanation concerning "the how" and "the why" believers are freed from sin. **These verses emphatically state that sin no longer reigns in the life of believers.** Before moving forward, take a few minutes to prayerfully review Romans 6:1-11.

2. Read Romans 6:1. Thinking biblically, why is continuing to sin not the best option to reveal the greatness of God's grace? How is it better revealed? If possible, cite a verse to share in support of your answer.

3. What would "sinning more" accomplish? To what does sin lead?

4. In Romans 6:2, God declares that you have died to sin. How is that working for you? Do you genuinely feel that you are dead to sin? You are invited to share your thoughts.

5. You were baptized into the newness of life. What is that? In your own words, define "newness of life."

6. You are no longer a slave to sin. How was this accomplished? Record the **keywords or phrases** in Romans 6:6-9.

v. 6 _____

v. 7 _____

v. 8 _____

v. 9 _____

7. Read Romans 6:10. What do you think it means to *live to God*? Are you living to God? If not, what's your plan to get back on track?

8. Many biblical characters lived to glorify God. Scripture has pulled back the curtain and given us a visual. It has provided believers a front-row seat into the saints of old "living to the glory of God" and "the just living by faith." Your life provides a visual image as well. What does it reflect? Remember, you may be the only bible that nonbelievers ever read. Since that's the case, answer the following questions.

a. What five attributes/characteristics that glorify God would you like them (others) to see from your life? Thinking biblically, list them in the order of significance, beginning with the most essential attribute or characteristic.

1._____

2._____

3._____

4._____

5._____

♥ <u>**Heart-Check For Today**</u>.

b. Who is your favorite biblical hero or heroine? As you consider their life and faithfulness, what about their journey speaks most to your heart? How has their story recently inspired you, encouraged your faith, or impacted your day-to-day life?

9. Read Romans 6:11. You are dead to sin. In your words, what does that mean?

10. From Romans 6:1-11, Paul urges us, by faith, to embrace all that God's Word had revealed. For refreshing, reflection, and reinforcement, let's examine an excerpt from Paul's letter to the church at Ephesus. Read and complete the following passage from Ephesians 2:1-10 (NKJV).

As you complete today's lesson, ask God to make these passages alive in you!

"And _____ *He made* _____, who were _____ in trespasses and _____, **2** in which you once _____ according to the course of this _____, according to the _____ of the power of the air, the _____ who now _____ in the sons of _____, **3** among whom also _____ all once conducted _____ in the _____ of our flesh, fulfilling the _____ of the _____ and of the _____, and were by nature children of _____, just as the others. **4** _____ _____, who is rich in _____, because of His great _____ with which He loved _____, **5** even when we were _____ in trespasses, made us _____ together with Christ (by _____ you have been _____), **6** and raised _____ up together, and made _____ sit together in the heavenly _____ in _____ _____, **7** that in the ages to come He might show the exceeding _____ of His _____ in *His* _____ toward us in Christ Jesus. **8** For by _____ you have been saved through _____, and that not of yourselves; *it is* the _____ of God, **9** not of _____, lest anyone should boast. **10** For we are His _____, created in Christ Jesus for _____ _____, which God prepared _____ that we should _____ in them" (Ephesians 2:1-10).

Tomorrow's lesson will invite you to respond to God's word. As you conclude today's lesson, you are invited to reflect on all that God has accomplished on your behalf - through Jesus - because He loves you! Meditate on the goodness of God.

Remember to make it personal because Christ died for you and has loved you with everlasting love. There is no love, like the love of Jesus. Who else would die for you? It's a sacrificial love that is without end and asks nothing in return. It loves you, just as you are - no matter what!

Embrace Jesus today and give thanks to God the Father for His plan to save you! Rejoice! You are loved and at liberty to sin no more!

Lesson 7: Dead To Sin And Alive In Christ
Romans 6:1-14

Day Five: **Respond**. Prayerfully read Romans 6:1-14.

Memory Verse: "Therefore we were buried with Him through baptism into death, that just as Christ was raised from the dead by the glory of the Father, even so we also should walk in newness of life" (Romans 6:4).

Romans 6:1-11 identified the spiritual aspects of our fellowship with Christ in His death and resurrection. Yesterday, we identified this as our justification. In other words, through this fellowship – by faith - we were justified and presently enjoy right standing before God. We are not guilty! When God looks at the redeemed, He sees Jesus. Romans 6:12-14 highlights the practical effects or by-products of that association and fellowship. In response to all that Christ has accomplished on your behalf, you are obedient to Him and live to honor Him with your life. One might say these verses pinpoint our response. What's the appropriate response? It's right living or living to righteousness. As was stated in an earlier lesson, "You belong to Him, inside and out!" Your obedience responds in love and devotion, never out of obligation, self-righteousness, or a sense of duty. Over time, you look more and more like Jesus, by His grace and for His glory – that's **sanctification**. Let's review our definition from Dr. Wayne Grudem. Sanctification is "a progressive work of God and man that makes us more and more free from sin and more like Christ in our actual lives."[5]

Today's verses introduce the **doctrine of sanctification**. In Romans 6:12 - Romans 8, we will study and embrace the aspects of practical living for Christ in the here and now. These passages identify the primary components of the "just living by faith." It is interesting to note that the "useful or profitable life" is incumbent upon all that Christ has accomplished through His death and resurrection. Apart from that, you would be just as hopeless and helpless as ever - doomed and eternally separated from God. Remember, there can never be sanctification without justification. As we begin our study, keep this statement in the back of your mind. "Let the redeemed of the Lord say so, and then live accordingly!" Enjoy the study.

---

[5] Grudem, W. A. (2004). *Systematic theology: an introduction to biblical doctrine* (p. 1253). Leicester, England; Grand Rapids, MI: Inter-Varsity Press; Zondervan Pub. House.

1. Read Romans 6:12. Paul begins by calling our justification into account. In your own words, what is Paul saying?

2. From the Greek, Romans 6:12 appears in the imperative mood. It's a command which encourages us to become what we are. As His children, we must step into who God has destined us to be. After all, His work is sufficient – it does not lack in any measure. He said, "It was finished," and He meant it! Even though you may not feel quite there in the moment, He sees the new and improved you – even now! Thinking biblically, why would this be an important statement for Paul to make?

3. What is your mortal body?

4. a. Using a bible, bible dictionary, or concordance, define *lust(s)*.

b. List the first five lusts that come to mind.

1.
2.
3.
4.
5.

5. Read Romans 6:13. In this passage, Paul notes two important presentations of our members. One highlights what we do, and the other highlights what we don't do - in our members. From the verse, complete these thoughts.

a. Define who/what your members are?

b. Do not present...

c. But, present yourselves...

d. And your members…

6. In a one-sentence response, what is "righteousness to God?"

7. In the newness of life, we partner with God to live to glorify Him and not ourselves. We should live at God's disposal. Once saved, His purposes become our purposes, and we have eternity in view. Therefore, we have a choice, and that choice is "whom we shall serve." A Scottish Quaker who lived in the 1600s said it like this. "We are faced with the tremendous alternative of making ourselves *weapons in the hand of God or weapons in the hand of sin* [emphasis added]." What is the best way to make yourself a weapon in the hand of God? Please cite a verse in support of your answer.

8. "Under" what do you live, instead of the law? _____

9. Define *grace* in your own words.

10. Complete Romans 6:14. For _____ shall not have _____ over you, for _____ are not under _____ but under grace.

In Christ, you have died to sin and are alive to God. (Review Romans 6:10-11.) As believers, we are challenged and inspired each day to live from that point of view. Every day we have choices to make and should operate from our newfound position, which is a place of profound honor and privilege. After all, only the redeemed of God have this opportunity. Rejoice! You belong to Jesus; you are the Beloved's, and the Beloved is yours! Pause a few minutes to praise God, for He alone is worthy!

You are hidden with Christ in God. Essentially, Romans 6:4 says in newness of life, we are alive to God! It seems only logical that if you are dead to sin in your body, its members are dead to sin as well. Therefore, sin has lost its hold over you. Reckon it so! You are free from that equal opportunity menace and nondiscriminatory evil force that kills and destroys. It no longer has access to any of your members. That's everything, including your thoughts, ideas, and motives. In the newness of life, you don't fulfill the deeds of the flesh. It is accomplished in the spiritual, but generally speaking - it's a little harder in the natural. That's because your "will" plays a leading role in your success. You either "will" or "won't" yield to God. We are stubborn people. It's linked to our inheritance from Adam and that old original sin. That's where the reckoning comes in. We must come into agreement with God, reckon it so, and respond accordingly. Faith must rise up! You are a new creation in Christ Jesus. Abandon it all to God, let go and walk in victory and newness of life. It is accomplished! It is finished! The time has come to reckon it so! What will your choice be moving forward? Will your life be a weapon in the hand of God? Yes_____ or No_____

Words of Jesus
"Let not your heart be troubled; you believe in God, believe also in Me" (John 14:1).

Lesson 8: Slaves To Righteousness
Romans 6:15-23

Day One: **Read**. Prayerfully read Romans 6:15-23

Memory Verse: "For the wages of sin is death, but the gift of God is eternal life in Christ Jesus our Lord" (Romans 6:23).

1. To set the tone for today's lesson, Paul asks another rhetorical question. What is it? Read and record Romans 6:15 below.

2. What is Paul's emphatic two-word response? _____!

3. Everyone has a master. You either serve God or sin - there are no other options. Paul declares that we are slaves to the one we obey. Complete Romans 6:16 below.

Do you not know that to whom you present yourselves _____ to _____, _____ are that one's _____ whom _____ _____, whether of _____ *leading* to _____, or of _____ *leading* to _____?

4. From the passage above, it's evident that we are slaves to whom we obey. Every believer's life tells a story of obedience. As grace through faith moves us from slaves to sin to slaves of God, our allegiance is transferred. It becomes obvious to everyone whom we obey. In newness of life, our joyful obedience confirms and testifies of your newfound freedom in Christ. What does Jesus teach us about obedience? Read and record John 14:15 below.

John 14:15

5. Read Romans 6:16. Obedience leads to:

6. Nonbelievers live under the misconception that they are free. They erroneously assume that allegiance to Christ would end their freedom. "These" are deceived, and slaves to sin, and the reality is this. They're the most bound and perhaps the most miserable people on earth. Sin begets sin and always leads to destruction and death - theirs! True liberty is a gift that only comes from God. He is the one giver of everything needed. What's that? Simply stated, it's freedom from sin and death in exchange for righteousness in Christ Jesus. That is life! As you come to faith, you exchange the old master for the One Master and the lover of your soul. Read Romans 6:17 and complete the following phrases, using the words from the verse.

Formerly you were:_____

How did the heart respond?_____

What did you obey?_____

7. **But God** is the most powerful two-word phrase in all of scripture, as the powerful life-changing phrase appears 43 times - sprinkled throughout both testaments. Watch this. Every time these words appear, God changes man's destiny, his course, or the projected outcome. In short, their destiny was charted until they collided with the love of God. **But God** infuses His love and mercy

into the story every time. His love always changes the circumstances and consequences. We were all headed one way until God's love intervened. God always had a plan to save you and change your destiny. To paraphrase Romans 6:17, Paul says, "Thanks be to God, even though you were dead in your sin, when your heart obeyed, you were delivered into the doctrine of grace." When it pleased God, He revealed His Son in you, and you were saved. Because this is so important, let's take a closer look. For clarity, 1). Read and record the "But God" phrase from each passage, and 2). What did God change in each verse?

Genesis 50:20 -

Romans 5:8 -

1 Corinthians 1:27 -

8. How has God changed your course, your destiny, and your projected outcome? Please highlight your most memorable **"But God"** encounter below. You're invited to share how a loving God intervened on your behalf.

9. From Romans 6:18, we discover a summary thought in light of all that Christ has done. What do you become and why?

10. Thinking biblically, answer the following:

   a. What does it mean to be a slave to righteousness?

   b. What does it mean to you personally?

c. What challenge(s) does this pose in your life?

d. When Jesus triumphed over the enemy on the Mount of Temptation, He used God's Word. It was enough! (See Matthew 4:1-11.) Although He could have called in heavenly aide, He won the battle with the strength and power of God's Word. Watch this. The truth of God's Word was more than enough to not only sustain and undergird (support) Him, but it was enough to defeat the enemy as well. How have you handled the enemy's opposition and attacks?

Lesson 8: Slaves To Righteousness
Romans 6:15-23

Day Two: **Research**. Review Romans 6:15-23.

Memory Verse: "For the wages of sin is death, but the gift of God is eternal life in Christ Jesus our Lord" (Romans 6:23).

Using a bible, bible dictionary, or concordance, define the following *keywords*.

a. *slave(s)* vv. 16, 17, 18, 19, 20

b. *obey, obeyed, obedience* vv. 16, 17

c. *uncleanness* v. 19

d. *lawlessness* v. 19

II. Read the following **key phrases.**

not under law v. 1

    <u>not</u> - *ouk* - An absolute negative; nay, neither, never, no

    <u>under</u> - *hypo* - Subject to; under; under the control of; under obligation to law –

    <u>law</u> - *noms* – From Eerdmans Bible Dictionary: "**law** Heb. *tôrâ;* also *miṣwâ* 'commandment,' *dābār* 'word, commandment,' *ḥōq* 'statute, decree,' *mišpaṭ* 'ordinance, judgment'; Aramaic. *dāṯ* 'law, regulation.' " Note: Law has the same meaning In Greek and Hebrew.

Galatians 5:18

under grace v. 15 –

    <u>under</u> - *hypo* - Subject to; under; under the control of; under obligation to

    <u>grace</u> - *charis* - At its core meaning, we find God's unmerited favor toward humanity, especially His people. It was first realized through the covenant and is fulfilled in and through Jesus Christ. According to various bible commentaries, referencing its new testament usage, ***grace*** holds a key position in all of Paul's letters. According to his new testament usage, Paul confirms that 1). God's grace is inseparable from His love expressed in Jesus Christ. And 2). That divine grace is dispensed only by God. Therefore, as believers, we conclude that we live only under an obligation to God's unmerited and undeserved favor – His grace. We find at the

center of this *divine grace* God expresses His unfailing love for humanity by sending a Savior named Jesus.

John 3:16

slaves of sin v. 17 –
   <u>slave</u> - ***doulas*** - Literally a person under an obligation to render total obedience or allegiance to a master.
   <u>sin</u> - ***hamartia*** - At its core meaning, sin is any failure to conform to God's moral law in act, attitude, or nature. Therefore, "slaves of sin" live under an obligation, obedience, or total allegiance to its master sin, which is any failure to conform to God's view, as expressed through His word. Complete 2 Peter 2:19 and John 8:34 below.

"While they promise them _____, they themselves are _____ of _____ [sin]; for by whom a person is overcome, by him also he is brought into _____" (2 Peter 2:19).

"Jesus answered them, 'Most assuredly, I say to you, whoever commits _____ is a _____ _____ _____ '" (John 8:34).

slaves of God v. 22
   <u>slave</u> - ***doulas*** - Literally a person under an obligation to render total obedience or allegiance to a master.
   <u>God</u> - ***theos*** - *From the Greek-English Lexicon of the NT* "*the one supreme supernatural being as creator and sustainer of the universe—'God.'*" There is none other. God is the lover of your soul, the great I AM, the Creator of heaven and earth, the Alpha and the Omega - the everlasting God!

Romans 11:36

members as slaves of uncleanness v. 19

member - *melos* - Literally a part of the body - "body part; member." *Member* may be rendered by an expression meaning *things of the body*.

slave - *doulas* - a person who is under an obligation to render total obedience or allegiance to a master.

uncleanness - *akatharsia* - *From the Greek-English Lexicon of the NT "the state of moral impurity, especially in relation to sexual sin—'impurity, immorality, filthiness.'"*

Therefore, members as slaves of uncleanness mean things of the body or body parts that render total obedience and allegiance to moral impurity and filthiness, especially as it relates to sexual sin. Read and complete Romans 1:24 and Galatians 5:19 below.

"Therefore God also gave them up to _____, in the _____ of their _____, to dishonor their _____ among themselves,..." (Romans 1:24).

Now the works of the flesh are evident, which are: adultery, fornication, _____, lewdness,..." (Galatians 5:19)

members as slaves of righteousness for holiness v. 19

member; slaves - See above definitions.

righteousness - *dikaiosunē* - *From the Greek-English Lexicon of The NT, "the act of doing what God requires, doing what is right."* Eerdmans Bible Dictionary has simplified the meaning of righteousness by touching every nuance of its meaning. It states, *"Within the new eschatological focus "righteousness" in the New Testament can stand for the salvation that God brings in the new age* [Christ's death on Calvary was a righteous act]; *the ethical possibilities brought by this salvation* [Because of Christ's sacrificial and propitiatory work (doing what was pleasing to God; regaining God's favor) on the cross, believers have right standing before God - we are justified; declared not guilty], *and the life of God's kingdom, now revealed* [the fruit of righteousness or right living]."

In summary, Paul's teaching reflects every nuance of righteousness. For clarity, complete the following.

1. Christ is our righteousness. Read 1 Corinthians 1:30. In addition to becoming wisdom from God, what else did Christ become for us? Be specific.

2. The progressive revelation of God's righteousness takes place in the gospel of Christ. Prayerfully review Romans 1:16-17. It is the thesis statement of the book of Romans.

3. Righteousness is received as a gift. Prayerfully read Romans 5:17.

   a. What reigned "through the One?"

   b. What will reign in life through the One, Jesus Christ?

4. Read Romans 5:1. The righteousness of God, which is distinguished from human righteousness, is identified in God's action for the salvation of humanity.

How are you justified?

5. Read 2 Corinthians 5:21. Through the sacrifice of Christ, all believers "become the "righteousness of God in Him."

What did Christ become for us, and why?

6. Christ's cross is the act of righteousness that saves. Prayerfully read Romans 5:18.

holiness - **_hagios_** - at its root meaning, this holiness is desiring the things of God; things that are pure, sacred, blameless. A literal translation would be "slaves of righteousness for sanctifying." From Romans 6:19, sanctification was the goal of righteousness. From the original language, the phrase "righteousness for holiness" occurs in the accusative case, verifying and confirming the author's intent. The phrase is the direct object of the verb "present." Righteousness leads to holiness, in contrast with sin, which leads to wickedness. You may recall from last week's lesson, the process of believers being sanctified is an ongoing, progressive work of God, with our participation (emphasis added). That sanctification makes us more and more like Jesus. This progressive, participatory work will continue throughout your life. It will not be complete until you stand in His presence. Read the promises of Matthew 5:10, Colossians 3:22-24, and Romans 8:2. Record Romans 8:2 below.

Romans 8:2

Lesson 8: Slaves To Righteousness
Romans 6:15-23

Day Three: **Receive**. Review Romans 6:15-23.

Memory Verse: "For the wages of sin is death, but the gift of God is eternal life in Christ Jesus our Lord" (Romans 6:23).

1. Review Romans 6:19. From this passage, what does Paul mean by the "weakness of your flesh?"

2. Make it personal. What is the weakness of your flesh? You are invited to share.

3. How are you winning the battle over your flesh? What suggestion would you make to others?

4. Notice in Romans 6:19 that "lawlessness leads to more lawlessness." Sin always begets more sin! Over time we become more and more desensitized to sin. Where does it lead? Where has it lead in your own life, presently or in times past? You are invited to share a testimony to encourage the faith of others. Don't forget to include how God has redeemed you from this circumstance, situation, mindset, or lifestyle. He is a gracious redeemer and is faithful to redeem us every day!

5. When temptation, self-destructive deeds, behavior, or thoughts creep in, stop and pray. When our flesh is weak, God's help is available. Read and record the promise of Romans 8:26 below.

6. Let's take a closer look at *lawlessness*. Among Bible scholars, it is agreed that lawlessness is *to behave with complete disregard for laws and regulations as set forth by society*. According to God's Word, *lawlessness* means *living or acting with complete disregard for His [God's] laws*. In no particular order, please list six lawless things that come to mind. If you are studying in a group, this should make for a lively discussion.

1.

2.

3.

4.

5.

6.

♥ Heart-Check For Today.

We cannot leave our discussion of lawlessness vs. righteousness without giving attention to Paul's word-choice from Romans 6:19. Notice the words "presented" and "present." In

Greek, the verb, **paristēmi** means *to make available, to provide*. From the verse, Paul explains the participation of our will. In essence, he firmly declares, "you have made available or provided your members for use to either lawlessness and sin or righteousness." From the original language, we find the active participation of our will is embedded within the word. It assures us that every decision we make involves our active participation for "good or evil."

The choice is yours! Look at that again. It requires your will, not your husbands, your children's, or your neighbor's. We can conclude by agreeing before a believer falls into sin or engages in sin, he or she makes a conscious decision. That's what Paul says in this passage. Romans 6 has primarily focused on knowing what Christ has achieved on your behalf, reckoning it as a done deal within your life, and then yielding accordingly. You know, you reckon, and you yield! Romans 6 challenges believers to "present" their members as slaves of righteousness for holiness!

As you receive God's Word into your hearts, prayerfully answer the following questions.

7. Since you have a choice, "will you" or "won't you," decide to yield to God?

8. Can you think of an area of your life that you are unwilling to trust to God? If so, what is it, and what is holding you back?

9. Even though you will be tempted in this life, God has given us many promises for victory in His Word. Please read the referenced verses, and follow the instructions below.

   a. Read and record 1 Corinthians 10:13

   b. For further reinforcement, prayerfully read John 16:33, 1 John 1:9, and 1 Corinthians 15:57. Which one of these verses most speaks to your heart and why?

10. Suggested For Group Participation:

   a. We are not on this journey alone. If you are doing this study in a group setting, will you take the opportunity to pray for a fellow sojourner? Turn to a partner now and pray words of victory and encouragement over her life. We need one another; we are much better together!

b. If you are doing this study alone, you are invited to record a personal prayer of victory below. The choice if yours! Rejoice in Jesus! Receive the victory in your heart today. He has done it. Reckon it so and yield to Him. Today, you can know victory and present your members as slaves to righteousness for holiness, by His grace and for His glory.

Lesson 8: Slaves To Righteousness
Romans 6:15-23

Day Four: **Reflect**. Prayerfully review Romans 6:15-23.

Memory Verse: "For the wages of sin is death, but the gift of God is eternal life in Christ Jesus our Lord" (Romans 6:23).

1. Read Romans 6:20. What occurred when you were a slave to sin?

2. Thinking biblically, what does it mean to be "*free*" in regard to righteousness?

♥ <u>**Heart-Check For Today**</u>.

3. Review Romans 6:20-21. Paul poses an essential question in verse 21. What about the fruit? This verse invites you to recall and consider the shameful fruit that your old life most assuredly produced. This passage confirms that apart from Christ, we all bear rotten or bitter fruit. It's a natural by-product of our hopeless, helpless, and sinful state. Thanks to God, believing in Jesus has changed everything, including your eternal destiny. Rejoice! You have "right standing" before God, presently, and anticipate an eternity worshiping and praising God. Write a short prayer of thanksgiving below.

4. In light of Romans 6:20, let's examine some contrasts that define most before and after stories. Reflecting on your journey, complete the "After Christ" portion of the chart.

Before Christ

lies and deception
lack of love
anger; hostility
lack of control
anxiety; fear
hatred; murder
stealing; covetousness

After Christ

5. In newness of life, we all have a victory story! Read Romans 6:21-22. We are set free from sin's bondage. We have become slaves of God. What does it mean to be "slaves of God?"

6. Most assuredly, there are benefits to freedom from sin and becoming slaves to God. Prayerfully consider your own life. Using descriptive words, describe how you have benefited?

7. Review Romans 6:21. If you remain unrepentant, what's at the end of bad fruit?

8. Believers are encouraged to grow in righteous living. We should long for righteousness and hate sin. A believer who does not desire holiness is alarming. The author of Hebrews agrees with Paul. A life of holiness is our desired end - it is the goal. Moreover, it's pleasing to God. Read the inspirational words of Hebrews 12:14-17, and record the instructions of verse 14 below. What does this verse confirm?

9. a. Record the words of Jesus from Matthew 5:6 below.

b. Thinking biblically, how will you be filled?

We conclude today's study with a powerful and expressive excerpt from *John Gill's Exposition of the Entire Bible* by John Gill [1746-63]. Mr. Gill was a 17th-century theologian, Puritan Pastor, Bible scholar, and expositor. Part of his commentary from Matthew 5:6 is quoted below:

after righteousness -

"... the justifying righteousness of Christ, which is imputed by God the Father, and received by faith. To hunger and thirst after this, supposes a want of righteousness, which is the case of all men; a sense of want of it, which is only perceived by persons spiritually enlightened; a discovery of the righteousness of Christ to them, which is made in the Gospel, and by the Spirit of God; a value for it, and a preference of it to all other righteousness; and an earnest desire after it, to be possessed of it, and found in it; and that nothing can be more grateful than that, because of its perfection, purity, suitableness, and use: happy souls are these..."

for they shall be filled –

"...with that righteousness, and with all other good things, in consequence of it; and particularly with joy and peace, which are the certain effects of it: or, 'they shall be satisfied,' that they have an interest in it; and so satisfied with it, *that they shall never seek for any other righteousness, as a justifying one, in the sight of God; this being full, perfect, sufficient, and entirely complete* [Emphasis added]."

10. Sin always exhausts itself and leads to death! Paul concludes Romans 6 with passionate words which assure believers that sin is deadly, but we receive the greatest gift available when we come to faith – eternity - and life in Christ Jesus our Lord.

"For the wages of sin *is* death, but the gift of God *is* eternal life in Christ Jesus our Lord" (Romans 6:23).

For reinforcement, complete the beautiful words of Jesus from Matthew 7:13-14 below.

"Enter by the _____ gate; for wide *is* the gate and _____ *is* the way that leads to _____, and there are many who go in by it. 14 Because _____ *is* the _____ and _____ *is* the way which leads to _____, and there are _____ who find it."

Lesson 8: Slaves To Righteousness
Romans 6:15-23

Day Five: **Respond**. Review Romans 6:15-23.

Memory Verse: "For the wages of sin is death, but the gift of God is eternal life in Christ Jesus our Lord" (Romans 6:23).

1. The beginning of the wonderful work of sanctification is noted in Romans 6:18. Did you catch it? Review the verse. In your own words, what does it say? What does it mean? How will you respond?

   It says:

   It means:

   I will respond:

2. This week, we examined "righteousness." Biblical righteousness, of course, is the act of doing what God requires. Romans 6:19 connects "slaves of righteousness" to holiness. In your own words, what does Paul saying in verse 19?

3. Romans 6 provides the best scriptural evidence of your spiritual transformation from death to life. What's the stunning conclusion? Sin leads to death, but God's gift of righteousness leads to life! (See Romans 6:23.) To better understand this miracle, you are invited to review the passages of Romans 6 to track your transformation. Although everyone's conversion is unique, the spiritual process is the same. The six phrases below highlight that spiritual process. In your opinion, which verse from the twenty-three passages of Romans 6 best expresses the **"We/We're"** statements listed below? Record the appropriate verse number in a-f. You are invited to share and discuss your answers.

a. **We** walk...v. _____

b. **We're** alive... v. _____

c. **We're** living under...v._____

d. **We're** slaves to...v. _____

e. **We're** set free...v._____

f. **We're** recipients of God's gift... v. _____

4. As you bring your study of Romans 6 to a conclusion, rest in the assurance that you are alive to God in Christ Jesus. God's word always confirms itself! Paul echoes this teaching in his letter to the church at Ephesus. For reinforcement, prayerfully complete Ephesians 2:4-7 NIV.

"But because of his great _____ for us, God, who is rich in _____, made us _____ _____ _____ even when we were _____ in transgressions—it is by _____ you have been saved. And God _____ us up with Christ and _____ us with him in the heavenly realms in _____ _____, in order that in the coming ages he might show the incomparable _____ of his _____, expressed in his _____ to us in Christ Jesus" (Ephesians 2:4-7). NIV

5. Notice in Romans 6:19 that "lawlessness leads to more lawlessness." Sin always begets more sin! Over time we become more and more desensitized to sin. Where does it lead? Where has it lead in your own life, presently or in times past? You are invited to share a brief testimony to encourage the faith of others. Don't forget to include how God has redeemed you from this circumstance, situation, mindset, or lifestyle. He is a gracious redeemer and is faithful to redeem us every day!

6. Thinking biblically, complete each phrase below to outline your journey of Romans 6:22-23. Take note: All who come to faith take this same path.

You believed and were freed from sin, but enslaved to _____; which

Leads to a life that bears _____ _____ _____; which Displays your _____ (hint: a spiritual work that occurs as a result of our _____); which leads to our ultimate goal and destiny which is _____ life.

7. As you prayerfully consider Romans 6, remember that our nature requires us to serve a master – we all do. With that thought in mind, consider these contrasts in Romans 6.

You serve one master, it's either:

_____ or _____ v. 16

8. Prayerfully review Romans 6:23. It appears that sin is a poor "paymaster." What are its wages? What does that mean in light of eternity?

As you receive God's word into your heart, make it personal. Know and acknowledge all that Christ has accomplished on your behalf. Then you must believe it is accomplished and reckon it so. In other words, you must believe with all your heart, mind, soul, and strength that it is complete on your behalf. Then, yield your life to God. Remember, Christ died for you!

In the newness of life, you are at liberty to obey. Faith in Jesus always leads to obedience. As bible students, we pause to recall our definition of *biblical faith*, which is *confident* **obedience** *to God's word despite the circumstances or consequences.* As a reminder, review Romans 1:5 and Romans 16:26 to encourage your faith-filled obedience.

♥ Heart-Check For Today.

Will you yield your life to Jesus? Will you walk in obedience to the faith? Noted pastor and theologian Dietrich Bonhoeffer said concerning obedience and faith, "Only the believing obey, only the obedient believe." Bonhoeffer knew the advancement of Christianity would come at a price as true discipleship always does. Who was Bonhoeffer? He was a German pastor and anti-Nazi dissident who publicly opposed Hitler and the extermination of the Jews. He preached and talked against Nazism at every opportunity. He never feared standing up for what was right – that all men are made in God's image and equal in God's sight. In an effort to bring the war to an end, he joined a group that plotted to assassinate Hitler, although their attempts were futile. Ultimately, he was jailed for these acts. After 18 months in prison, he was transferred to the Flossenbürg Concentration Camp. There he remained until he was martyred for his faith on April 9, 1945. Bonhoeffer was 39 at the time of his hanging. Like Jesus, he met his end hanging on a tree naked and unashamed. These were his last words. "This is the end, for me, the beginning of life."

Bonhoeffer's most widely-read work, *The Cost of Discipleship,* has been challenging and inspiring believers since its publication in 1937. It begins: "Cheap grace is the mortal enemy of our church. Our struggle today is for costly grace." It's apparent that Bonhoeffer despised lukewarm Christianity – to him, there was no such thing. He lived like he died – honoring Jesus with his life. His end testifies to his teaching that being a true disciple of Jesus will cost you everything. Bonhoeffer's faith never wavered. Until his death, he remained obedient to the faith!

Words of Jesus

"Jesus said to him, 'I am the way, the truth, and the life.
No one comes to the Father except through Me' " (John 14:6).

Lesson 9: A Portrait Of Marriage
Romans 7:1-13

Romans Road Map. You will deal with the issue of sin throughout your life. For believers, the question becomes, "After salvation, what is my relationship to God's law since I no longer live under the law, but under grace?" Paul's teaching of Romans 6 makes it abundantly clear that living under grace is never a license to sin. Instead, as new creatures, we are to walk victoriously and in the newness of life. Romans 7 will address our relationship to sin. Believers should be encouraged by their new status and the power of life that reigns within them. What's that? Of course, it's Christ in you, the hope of glory! (See Colossians 1:27.) Romans 7 assures all believers that righteousness (right living) is a possibility. Paul affirms that a "life of righteousness to holiness" is not only possible - it's doable! Believers can bear the fruit of Christ, which not only glorifies God but pleases Him as well. Moving forward, Lessons 9 & 10 will highlight, explain, and conclude that believers are dead to the law just as they are dead to sin.

In Part Two of our study, we will continue learning about our relationship with the law. Lesson 11 will highlight what we've studied in Romans 1-6, and Lessons 12-20 will continue to train us in righteousness as we learn to walk in the power of God's Spirit. Paul has much to share from this beloved epistle. Before we begin Romans 7, let's look forward to what awaits us as we conclude Part One of our study.

A Breakdown of Romans 6 – 8:1-4

We are no longer living under condemnation of the law - Romans 7:1-6 (Lesson 9)

The law convicts believers and unbelievers of sin - Romans 7:7-13 (Lesson 9)

The law cannot deliver us from sin - Romans 7:14-25 (Lesson 10)

A Romans Review – An Overview of Romans 1 – 6. (Lesson 11)*

Fulfilling the law by walking in the power of the Spirit - Romans 8:1-4 (Lesson 12)*

* Lessons 11-20 are found in: *To Rome With Love, Book Two.*

Day One: **Read**. Prayerfully read Romans 7:1-13

Memory Verse: "Therefore, my brethren, you also have become dead to the law through the body of Christ, that you may be married to another—to Him who was raised from the dead, that we should bear fruit to God" (Romans 7:4)

1. Review Romans 7:1. Who is Paul addressing, and what question does he ask?

2. Review Romans 7:2. What analogy does Paul present?

3. How long is a wife bound to her husband, and how is she released?

4. Review Romans 7:3. Why would she be called an adulteress? Be specific.

5. When is she not called an adulteress?

6. What is Paul's conclusion? Review and record Romans 7:4 below to reveal the answer.

Romans 7:4

7. Review Romans 7:4 and answer the following questions. Where possible, record the appropriate phrase from the verse.

   a. Through what means are you dead to the law?

   b. Who is the other to whom you may be married?

    c. For what purpose?

8. Read Romans 7:5. What happened when we were in the flesh? Be specific.

9. What were the results?

10. In your own words, what is *fruit to death*?

11. Romans 7:6 says that we are delivered from the law. Through what means? Be specific

12. Paul draws a stunning conclusion in the outcome. How should we serve?

Lesson 9: A Portrait Of Marriage
Romans 7:1-13

Day Two: **Research**. Prayerfully read Romans 7:1-13

Memory Verse: "Therefore, my brethren, you also have become dead to the law through the body of Christ, that you may be married to another—to Him who was raised from the dead, that we should bear fruit to God" (Romans 7:4).

I. Using a bible, bible dictionary, or concordance, define the following *keywords*.

a. *adulteress* v. 3

b. *covetousness* v. 7

II. Read the following *key phrases.*

those who know the law v. 1
   those who know - Paul is addressing the entire church at Rome. The Jews knew the law, and the Gentiles were informed. The Old Testament Law was not new.
   the law - In this verse, Paul is speaking of *the law* in general terms. He is speaking of the law's fundamental character rather than the Mosaic legislation of the law.

bound by the law v 2 -
>***bound*** - From the *Greek-English Lexicon of the New Testament*, "*bound* is to cause someone to be under the authority of someone or something else—'to restrict, to place under (the jurisdiction of).'"
>***the law*** - The commandments of God. Literally under the authority, jurisdiction, and/or restrictions of the law of God.

dead to the law v. 4 - From *The Greek-English Lexicon of the NT, dead* means "*to cease completely from activity, with the implication of extreme measures taken to guarantee such a cessation—'to stop completely, to cease completely.'* That is a figurative extension of the root word meaning *to deprive a person of life, with the implication of this being the result of condemnation by legal or quasi-legal procedures—'to kill, to execute.'*

Therefore, you purposely cease living 'according to and under the obligation, duty, or restriction of the law.'"

According to Colossians 3:5, what causes death? How might you live?

♥ Heart-Check For Today.

In Lessons 9 & 10, Paul will answer the probing question of Romans 6:15, "Shall we continue in sin because we are not under the law?" He concludes that people are dead to the law just as they are dead to sin. Romans 6:14 clearly states that you are not living under the law, but grace and sin (and sinning) no longer dominate you. Remember that living under the law required something of us for God; living under grace required we receive what God has done for us. Do you see the contrast?

bear fruit to God v. 4 - Everyone's life bears fruit, believers and nonbelievers alike. The question becomes what type of fruit? There are two options, fruit for good or fruit for evil. Notice from v. 4, believers are dead to the law, married to Jesus, and bearing fruit to God. In the newness of life, believers have new attitudes and new actions, and natural byproducts (fruit) embody their lives. They are found in the will of God, delight in pleasing God, testify of God, and celebrate God. Married to Jesus, our new lives are productive for God.

"But the fruit of the Spirit is _____, _____, _____, _____, _____, _____, _____, _____, _____.

Against such there is no law" (Galatians 5:22-23).

From that list would you say that you're bearing fruit to God?

we were in the flesh v. 5 - In the Bible, "*flesh*" has several uses. The word used in a "non-moral sense" describes man's physical being. When used in a "morally evil sense," it describes our unredeemed humanness - or the natural state of man. In this sense, *flesh* highlights the lingering fragments of the old self. In our humanness, remnants of *flesh* will remain and resurface in each believer until we stand before Christ - in our completeness. Romans 8:23.

In the flesh, generally speaking, references a person who operates in the sphere of fallen humanity. That would mean an unredeemed, unregenerate person. From *The Theological Dictionary of the New Testament* – "*believers have crucified the **sárx** or flesh. They enter a life that in Christ is determined by the relationship to God. Works of the flesh are illogical and call for recommitment. This life is not split up into single acts. It is one **érgon** (work) under one determination, sárx (flesh). <u>Believers are no longer building on the flesh but on Christ. This is what they are to achieve in the daily practice of the life of faith</u> [emphasis added].*"

Prayerfully review Romans 8:8-9 and answer the following:

  a. Who cannot please God?

b. If someone does not have the Spirit of Christ, what does that mean?

From Galatians 5:24, if you are Christ's, what have you crucified? Be specific.

fruit to death v. 5 - In contrast with *fruit to God*, this is deadly fruit! That is the fruit that leads to death, and sadly apart from salvation, it is the natural fruit. When sinful passions, pleasures, and pursuits prevail in one's life, there is only one outcome and only one destiny. That is spiritual death and separation from God presently, which leads to a second death and separation from God throughout eternity.

From Galatians 6:7-8:

a. What does man sow?_____

b. What does sowing in the flesh reap?_____

c. What does sowing in the Spirit reap?_____

oldness of the letter v. 6 - That means our old master, the law, and the commandments, that external, written code of dos and don'ts that no one could keep, except Jesus. They produced only hostility, condemnation, and guilt in the hearts of man. The law not only revealed sin but demanded action. Therein lies the problem — man's natural inclination rebels against the law as well as the lawgiver. "Self" hates authority and always desires to be its own master! Since the beginning, that has been man's problem, just like Adam and the original sin. We think we know better than God. We set ourselves up as God. We tragically serve ourselves and our desires, which lead to death and destruction rather than God and His desires, which lead to life.

Lesson 9: A Portrait Of Marriage
Romans 7:1-13

Day Three: **Receive**. Prayerfully review Romans 7:1-13

Memory Verse: "Therefore, my brethren, you also have become dead to the law through the body of Christ, that you may be married to another—to Him who was raised from the dead, that we should bear fruit to God" (Romans 7:4).

1. Is the law sin?

2. What is it, and what was its purpose? In your own words, describe the purpose of the law.

3. Review Romans 7:7. Paul makes it personal by using his testimony to define sin.

   a. How did Paul know sin?

b. Paul discovered something significant when the law said, "You shall not covet."

What did he discover?

4. Think back to your revelation of sin. Do you have a testimony like Paul's? What did God's word first reveal to you about sin?

Example: How and when did you come to agree with God about lying, stealing, adultery, etc.? When you realized that these things were sinful, you had a revelation of God's word, and you agreed with God. The enemy is defeated by the blood of the Lamb and the word of our testimony. (Revelation 12:11.) You are His witness, rejoice! From the foundation of the world, God had a plan to accomplish His will in and through your life, and it was rooted in love. You are invited to share a brief testimony of your revelation of sin.

5. From Romans 7:8, what does Paul say sin took the opportunity to accomplish?

6. How would you define all manner of evil desire?

7. Read Romans 7:9. What died apart from the law? Thinking biblically, why was it dead?

8. Romans 7:9 reveals that once Paul was *something* without the law. What was it?

9. What happened when the commandment came? Thinking biblically, what does that mean?

10. Poor Paul, he was deceived and died. How so? Record Romans 7:11

11. According to verse 11, you were deceived and died too! What does this mean to you?

12. Paul concludes in Romans 7:12. How does Paul describe the law and commandments? For your answer, record the "is" statement below.

13. Sin became exceedingly sinful, according to verse 13. Read the verse and, in your own words, describe what occurred when sin became exceeding sinful.

Lesson 9: A Portrait Of Marriage
Romans 7:1-13

Day Four: **Reflect**. Review Romans 7:1-13

Memory Verse: "Therefore, my brethren, you also have become dead to the law through the body of Christ, that you may be married to another—to Him who was raised from the dead, that we should bear fruit to God" (Romans 7:4).

1. Paul begins chapter 7 with a simple analogy. Read Romans 7:1-3 and answer the following:

	Who does the wife represent?_____

	Who does the husband represent?_____

2. A review of the memory verse confirms that:

believers are dead to the law through the _____ of _____.

It further states: that _____ may be _____ to another. To whom? To _____ who was _____ from the _____.

For what unique purpose? Be specific. Complete the verse below.

❤ *<u>Heart check For Today</u>*.

3. Through Jesus Christ, believers are dead to sin and the law. Sometimes, instead of living under grace, we allow old habits and mindsets to creep back in. If we believe that following the law indicates our spiritual growth or progress, we are being deceived. When this occurs, instead of

enjoying the liberty we have in Christ, we overwhelm ourselves with legalistic dos and don'ts. Can you recall a time when you overburdened yourself with performance or works instead of resting wholly in Christ's righteousness? Could it be that it is presently the case? Either way, you are invited to share

4. Legalism leads to many problems, self-righteousness heading the list! The law has absolutely no value in our justification. As a reminder, read and record Romans 3:20 below.

Romans 3:20

5. From Romans 3:20, what knowledge is revealed in the law?

6. In Romans 7, Paul assures us that the law did not save us. It did not set us apart or make us holy at the time of our regeneration or new birth. Nor does it grow us and mature us as believers. Nor does it help us demonstrate the character of God and His righteousness in our everyday lives.

As you recall the scriptural progression in Romans 7, complete the following statements.

a. Jesus is our representative, He died and _____ died with Him.

b. Through Jesus' death, our _____ debt was paid and forever satisfied by His blood on Calvary. That's all sin! Past, present, and future, including the eternal consequences of sin. Our Savior, Jesus, paid it all.

c. When He died, He _____ the law and ended all relationship to the law. We, too, are separated from the law by identifying with Jesus (believing in Jesus) and His sacrificial death on Calvary. Therefore, we are legally released from any obligation to the law.

d. We are released from our union with sin and are joined to another. Jesus! We are the bride of _____. We walk in the newness of life. Although the law still exists, it is a non-participant in our lives. Through Christ Jesus, we are free from sin and free from the law. Instead, we are obligated only to our new Master or husband.

7. You are obligated to your new Master! For reflection, read and review Romans 6:15-23 and complete the words from Romans 6:22-23.

"But now having been set _____ _____ _____, and having become slaves of _____, you have your fruit to holiness, and the end, _____ _____. For the wages of sin *is* _____, but the _____ of God *is* eternal _____ in _____ _____ our Lord" (Romans 6:22-23).

8. You are obligated to your new husband! For reflection, read and review Romans 7:1-6 and complete the words from the selected verses.

"Or do you not know, brethren (for I speak to those who know the law), that the law has dominion over a man as long as he lives? v.2 For the woman who has a husband is bound by the law to her husband as long as he lives. But if the husband dies, she is released from the law of her husband. v.3 So then if, while her husband lives, she marries another man, she will be called an adulteress; but if her husband dies, she is _____ _____ _____ _____, so that she is no adulteress, though she has married _____ man. v.4 Therefore, my brethren, you also have become dead to the law through the body of Christ, that you may be married to another—to _____ who was raised from the dead, that we should bear fruit _____ _____. v.5 For when we were in the flesh, the sinful passions which were aroused by the law were at work in our members to bear fruit to _____. v.6 But now we have been delivered from the _____, having _____ to what we were held by, so that we should _____ in the newness of the _____ and not in the oldness of the _____."

Before we move forward, note this. Paul illustrates two essential facts about the law in Romans 7:1-6 above. First, believers died to the law, and second, we are delivered from the law. In simple terms, that means that the law cannot exercise its authority over us. That is so very important. The law is not dead; we died, not the law. It still exists, but it has no hold - no authority - over us. Instead, because we believe in Jesus and His Spirit embodies us, we are empowered to walk in newness of life (Romans 6:4) and serve in newness of Spirit (Romans 7:6).

Lesson 9: A Portrait Of Marriage
Romans 7:1-13

Day Five: **Respond**. Review Romans 7:1-13

Memory Verse: "Therefore, my brethren, you also have become dead to the law through the body of Christ, that you may be married to another—to Him who was raised from the dead, that we should bear fruit to God" (Romans 7:4).

1. Life was the nucleus of the law. Its primary purpose was to bring life. According to Leviticus, **the law was not only central to life; but it was also** the way of life. The verse reads, *"You shall, therefore, keep My statutes and My judgments, which if a man does, he shall live by them; I am the Lord [emphasis added]." (Leviticus 18:5).* That's not the way it happened. We know because of sin, the law brought death instead.

Concerning the word *live,* we find the following information. In the Qal stem, Hebrew's simplest verb from, the primary meaning is "to live or have life." Additional information comes from *The Wordbook of the Old Testament "hāy – hāyâ - 'to live, have life, remain alive, sustain life, live prosperously, live forever. Also, be quickened, revive from sickness, discouragement, or even death.' "* Notice at the end of the definition, we find that *the law*, if followed, could also bring restoration of life from sickness, discouragement, or even death! That was the original plan; however, Paul says that something other occurred because there is sin in man. What happened? Review Romans 7:10-12. Record what happened from Romans 7:11 below.

Romans 7:11

2. Romans 7:11 reads, *"For sin, ...deceived me, and by it killed me [emphasis added]."* The word *deceived* in this passage adds an interesting element for discussion. Paul points out the enemy's ploy in converting the law (an instrument intended for life) into an instrument of death. *The*

Greek-English Lexicon of the NT " '*deceive - exapataō* - to cause someone to have misleading or erroneous views concerning the truth'—'to mislead, to deceive, deception.' " It is interesting to note in this exact form, meaning, and context *"deceive, deceived"* occurs six times in six passages, only through the words of Paul. Romans 7:11; 16:18, 1 Corinthians 3:18; 2 Corinthians 11:3; 2 Thessalonians 2:3; and 1 Timothy 2:14. Variations of the word, with nuances of this meaning, can be found elsewhere in the New Testament, including the books of Mark and James. For clarity, read 2 Corinthians 11:3 and 1 Timothy 2:14.

From 1 Timothy 2:14, who was not *deceived* and who fell into transgression (sin)?

3. Read and review Romans 7:7. In Pauline fashion, he answers his own question. Provide the answer to Paul's question by recording Romans 7:12 below.

Romans 7:12

4. Have you ever considered the law as being holy, just, and good? Or have you looked at it narrowly, thinking it was overbearing, burdensome, and condemning? It must be right and good; it's from God. How can anything from God not be so? One bible scholar noted this concerning Romans 7:12. "*Since the law is God's law, it must of necessity reflect the nature of God. The law of a holy God must be consistent with his holy nature. (See Isaiah 6:3.) A righteous God decrees righteous commandments. They are fair and make no unreasonable demands. The law is "good" because it intends the very best for people. In this entire discussion, Paul was not depreciating law as such.* **His point had been that law has been used by sin as an unwilling accomplice to bring about death.**"

By God's divine plan and authority, the law is consistent with God's holy nature. What is God's nature (character)? Record Isaiah 6:3 below.

Isaiah 6:3

5. For further clarity, let's examine God's nature and character through the revelation He shared with Moses at the giving of the Ten Commandments. Circle the underlined words or phrases which describe God.

Exodus 34:4-7 So he cut two tablets of stone like the first ones. Then Moses rose early in the morning and went up Mount Sinai, as the Lord had commanded him; and he took in his hand the two tablets of stone. Now the Lord descended in the cloud and stood with him there, and proclaimed the name of the Lord. And the Lord passed before him and proclaimed, v. 6 "The Lord, the Lord God, merciful and gracious, long-suffering, and abounding in goodness and truth, v. 7 keeping mercy for thousands, forgiving iniquity and transgression and sin, by no means clearing the guilty, visiting the iniquity of the fathers upon the children and the children's children to the third and the fourth generation."

6. Exodus 34:4-7 reveals God's character and identifies His work on the earth. In essence, this is God's job description, written by His very finger. Watch this. The overarching component is love - because God is love. (See 1 John 4:8; 16.) He is still revealing sin in the hearts and men. A loving God is still saving to the uttermost. Remember, apart from the revelation of sin, there is no repentance. Without repentance, there is no salvation. Without salvation, death is the result because sin always leads to death.

Review Exodus 34:4-7 from question 5 above. List the underlined character traits of God in the order of their importance to you personally. For group discussion, be prepared to share why you have selected this specific order.

1.

2.

3.

4.

5.

6.

7. Complete the words of Romans 7:13 below.

Has then what is _____ become _____ to me? Certainly not! But _____, that it might appear sin, was producing _____ in me through what is _____, so that _____ through the _____ might become exceedingly sinful.

8. In Romans 7:13, Paul brings clarity to Romans 7:9-12. In Pauline fashion, he poses another question, "Has what is good become death to me?"

Read and review Romans 7:9. Paul identifies the occasion or event of his death. What was it?

Paul identifies the instrument of his death. What was it? _____

9. Look closely at Romans 7:13. At first glance, the verse appears as a contradiction in terms. The "*good*," by definition, belongs to a different category from "*death*." Through the verse, Paul has clearly defined that it's the sin, not the commandment or the law, that has brought about his

death. It is the same with us. **We are dead because of our sin, not because of the law**. The law did not kill us, but our sinful nature did.

So what was the purpose of the law? The law was simply the instrument or schoolmaster God used in partnership with sin to accomplish its goal. It killed us because when the law revealed sin, we were doomed - we were all guilty! In the revelation of sin, we heard "don't," and sin became even more enticing to our sinful natures.

In the garden, Adam and Eve heard "don't," and the apple became irresistible, even though this was the only forbidden fruit! Like Adam, the very things that the law revealed as sinful lured us in – sin enticed us. We had to see; we had to feel; we had to touch. In essence, we had to push against God, so we continued in it. In our rebellious natural state, we are all predisposed or inclined to sin. It reaches back to Adam and the apple. In Adam, we find the root of our natural inclination or predisposition for sinful pleasures, passions, and pursuits. But as Paul explained, through this process, sin exposed itself and its character. It (sin) demonstrated how unspeakably sinful it is by using what was good to bring about death. Ladies, sin always leads to death. Thankfully, God had a plan to save us. Now, we are called to walk in the newness of life and bear fruit to Him. Read Romans 6:23 and record the last phrase of the verse below.

"...but the gift of God is _____."

How will you respond to God's powerful words of Romans 7:1-13? You are dead to sin and the law. You are married to another, the Lord Jesus! Rejoice! You are the bride of Christ. Let's take one last look at our memory verse, Romans 7:4. Pause and prayerfully read it aloud.

"Therefore, my brethren, you also have become dead to the law through the body of Christ, that you may be married to another—to Him who was raised from the dead, that we should bear fruit to God" (Romans 7:4).

As we conclude this lesson, think about the fruit of your life. What manner of fruit are you producing for God? Only you know the answer to this question. Remember, we have a good, faithful Father on our side. He is merciful, gracious, long-suffering, and abounding in goodness and truth. He desires that no man perish. That includes all those unsaved friends and relatives that you labor over in prayer. Remember this. When you pray for these, you do so in partnership with God. After all, He is the divine promise keeper, supreme above all others. There is none like our great and awesome God! He is keeping mercy for thousands, forgiving iniquity and transgression and sin, by no means clearing the guilty. He will deal will them in due season – He will prevail!

Vengeance Belongs To God.

Vengeance is mine sayeth the Lord! It has been said, "Trust vengeance to Him because the manner and timing of the repayment of man's wickedness is God's prerogative, for only He is just." Rest assured, the eye of God has not missed a thing! He is visiting the fathers' iniquity upon the children and the children's children to the third and the fourth generation. Although that looks harsh, there is divine mercy in that statement. Notice the contrast between three or four generations in light of the thousands who have received His mercy!

That "visitation of iniquity to the children and children's children" was not and is not a punishment to them. God is merely pointing out that we will suffer the consequences of our sins only for three or four generations.

Do you see God's mercy in that verse? The consequences could have been forever. That's reason for a great hallelujah shout! God is good! Just like Paul said, the law and the commandments are holy, just, and good. (Review Romans 7:12.)

God has good things planned for you!

"For I know the thoughts that I think toward you, says the Lord, thoughts of peace and not of evil, to give you a future and a hope. 12 Then you will call upon Me and go and pray to Me, and I will listen to you. 13 And you will seek Me and find *Me,* when you search for Me with all your heart. 14 I will be found by you, says the Lord...." (Jeremiah 29:11-14).What a rich promise. You are invited to close in prayer.

Words from Jesus
"Peace I leave with you, My peace I give to you; not as the world gives do I give to you. Let not your heart be troubled, neither let it be afraid" (John 14:27).

Lesson 10: The Struggle With Sin
Romans 7:14 - 25

Day One: **Read**. Prayerfully read Romans 7:14-25

Memory Verse: "O wretched man that I am! Who will deliver me from this body of death?

I thank God—through Jesus Christ our Lord!" (Romans 7:24-25).

Take note of the memory verse because these powerful words have been debated and talked about for years. What was Paul saying? What body of death, and what sin? Moreover, was Paul speaking in the present tense - post-salvation? Or was Paul allowing us to see the "old man" who died with Christ?

Most conservative theologians believe Paul was speaking post-salvation. That position will become more apparent as we move through our study. Where appropriate, we will examine what Paul is saying from the original language. Doing so will ensure correct exposition of Paul's inspired message from each verse. As you work through the study, you will discover why noted scholars of today hold this unified opinion concerning Paul's words of Romans 7:14-25. Enjoy the study.

1. Review Romans 7:14.

    a. What is the law?

    b. According to Paul, he is _____?

c. What does Paul imply by the words "sold under sin?"

2. From Romans 7:15, what does Paul not understand?

3. Review Romans 7:15. In simple terms, what is Paul saying? In your own words, explain these two phrases in the passage.

   a. "For what I will to do, that I do not practice;

   b. but what I hate, that I do."

4. Read Romans 7:16. What was "good" from this passage? Thinking biblically, what might that mean?

5. Read and review Romans 7:17.

    a. Who is sinning?

    b. Who is performing the action?

6. Prayerfully read Romans 7:18 and complete the following.

"For I know that _____ _____ (that is, in my _____) nothing _____ dwells; for to _____ is present with me, but _____ to _____ what is _____ I do not find" (Romans 7:18).

7. Read and review Romans 7:19. Record the verse below.

Romans 7:19

8. From Romans 7:19, we discovered the evil that Paul desires not to do is practiced - nonetheless. In verse 20, he explains how this occurs. Read and review Romans 7:20. Since it is "no longer I who do it," who does it, and how does it happen? Record the verse and underline your answer.

Romans 7:20

9. Read and review Romans 7:21. Paul *wills* to do good, even though something is present within him. What is it?

10. Read and review Romans 7:22. What does Paul's inward man feel about God's word? Give a one-word answer. _____

11. A war rages within Paul. Read and review Romans 7:23.

   a. In your own words, explain the war that rages within Paul.

   b. You are at war. How are you warring within? Please provide a brief example.

12. Read and review Romans 7:24-25. In bitterness of soul, Paul cries out for help! What question does he ask in verse 24? Be specific. Please record his exact words.

13. Read Romans 7:25. What were Paul's answer and accompanying conclusion? Record Romans 7:25 below.

Lesson 10: The Struggle With Sin
Romans 7:14 – 25

Day Two: **Research**. Review Romans 7:14-25

Memory Verse: "O wretched man that I am! Who will deliver me from this body of death? I thank God—through Jesus Christ our Lord!" (Romans 7:24-25).

I. Using a bible, bible dictionary, or concordance, define the following *keywords.*

   a. *spiritual* v. 14

   b. *carnal* v. 14

   c. *captivity* v. 23

II. Read the following **key phrases.**

is spiritual v. 14 - Its base meaning is "of the spirit; from the spirit." That means "something" (a message, an inspiration) is coming to us from God, from the Holy Spirit in the full measure of his Divine nature. The law is spiritual, for it has **a spiritual origin and a spiritual power**. As it pertains to man, evangelical Bible scholars agree that 'spiritual' (*πνευματικός*) *pneumatikos* means *being spiritual, having the characteristics of God's spirit with general reference to the higher nature of man being directly in touch with and influenced by God.* This word appears 26 times in 21 verses of the New Testament. Twenty of those verses come from Paul's writings. The remaining verse is found in 1 Peter 2:5. Complete the 1 Peter passage below.

"you also, as living stones, are being built up a _____ house, a holy priesthood, to offer up _____ _____ acceptable to _____ through Jesus Christ.

in my flesh v. 18, 25 - Although we examined "flesh" in last week's lesson, other nuances of its meaning must be noted. A broad definition comes from *The Greek-English Lexicon of the NT*. It states, *"flesh, σάρξ - sarx is the psychological aspect of human nature which contrasts with the spiritual nature. In other words, we are at odds - the spirit wars against our flesh. Here's a technical explanation. Those aspects of human nature which are characterized by or typically reflect human reasoning and desires are in direct conflict with those aspects of human thought and behavior that relate to God and the spiritual life."* In verse 18, sarx is translated "flesh" in the most commonly used versions of the Bible, except the New International Version (NIV) and the New Living Translation (NLT). Both of these versions translate sarx as "sinful nature." Notice in Romans 7:14, Paul describes himself as carnal, often translated *"unspiritual."* This word, *σάρκινος **sarkinos***, is also a form of the noun, ***sarx***, coming from the same root word. To expand or broaden the use of ***sarx*** and its meaning in scripture, this word, too, is generally translated "flesh" in the New Testament.

Bible scholars conclude ***sarx*** and its diverse uses in scripture can pose some challenges concerning translation and the original meaning of the word. They agree that the difficulty exists because the word ***sarx*** references several underlying meanings in the New Testament, as follows: 1). The physical dimension of our existence, that is, to our bodies; 2). As a synonym for the Greek word *soma*, which is translated by the word "body"; and 3). The nature of the whole man in his fallen state before his conversion.

For purposes of our study, we will agree that **sarx** and its multiple uses in scripture are crucial to understanding our **"sinful, fallen, or fleshly natures."** According to Paul, *sarx* or sin was warring within him. It's fighting within us as well. Theologian, pastor, and author, R. C. Sproul has noted, we don't get it right 100% of the time. He stated, *"But no Christian in this world achieves a 100% consistent desire to obey God only." Like Paul,* he concluded. Within us, we have a powerful desire leftover from our fallen nature. Let's take a quick look.

Although we're born again and possess God's Spirit (which means we have new natures, desires, inclinations, and attitudes, plus a new love for the things of God), we are not 100% obedient. In this life, our love is imperfect because of sin, the enemy, and the world. It is tainted with the human element (our inheritance from Adam), or a condition called sin. That new love that fills us is not perfect, it is not pure, and it is not yet completely realized in our lives. Every Christian will struggle to honor and obey God because their "old man" will war against their "new man" until the end. That is precisely the battle of every Christian, and Paul highlights it in Romans 7:14-25. That's the focus of our lesson. We can, therefore, conclude and agree that although it is our goal, it is humanly impossible 100% of the time. **Sarx** or sin will war or rage within us until we are complete and stand before Christ. Through personal confession and inspiration of the Holy Spirit, Paul has identified and defined the heart's cry of every believer. The struggle with sin has and will plague the heart of believers until Christ calls us home.

inward man v. 22 - inner being, innermost self - *From the Theological Dictionary of the NT, "inward man denotes the spiritual side of man, or the man himself in so far as he enjoys self-awareness, as he thinks and wills and feels. As such, "...man has access to divine revelation, can be conditioned by it and is open to its claim; yet the contradictory practical conduct which is determined by sin brings out the plight of man in the dualism [co-existing spirit and flesh] of his existence."*

"For I delight in the law of God according to the inward man" (Romans 7:22).

body of death v. 24 - identifies the believer's unredeemed humanness, which has its base of operation in the body. One Bible scholar suggested that Paul was perhaps referencing a custom of an ancient tribe near Tarsus. Paul, of Tarsus, would have been familiar with this practice. What was the tradition or custom? As punishment for murder, it was customary to tie the corpse of the victim to its murderer. It would remain there permanently, allowing its spreading decay to infect and execute the murderer slowly. It was considered a suitable punishment to fit the crime.

We find in *Elliott's Commentary For English Readers* "*that the body of this death is (the slave of sin and therefore the abode) of death.*" Paul knew it. He declares, "I'm a wretched man, and I beg for deliverance from this mortal body. But, I'm enslaved to my carnal (sensual and sexual) desires, plus every other sin, and death is inevitable. It's comingled and impossible to separate." *Paul has already declared, "...the wages of sin is death." (See Romans 6:23.)* Elliot continues, "*To complete this deliverance, the triple resurrection—ethical [moral], spiritual, and physical—is needed.*

Lesson 10: The Struggle With Sin
Romans 7:14 - 25

Romans Road Map. Although Paul's message of Romans 7:14-25 appears bleak at first glance, it has a glorious end! It is the same with us. Even though we're frail and sinful and live in a fallen world, we, too, anticipate a glorious end! And we shall have it because it's promised! One day soon, this life will be over, and we will be in the presence of the Lord. It's the product of our faith, which is "the substance of things hoped for and the evidence of things not seen." (See Hebrews 11:1.) We've believed and hoped in Christ for salvation, the surety of pardon, and the promised resurrection. Because we've put our faith in Christ - alone - we will realize this marvelous victory. Rejoice, heaven, and eternity with Jesus is your destiny!

Even though we're headed to heaven, we're not there yet! Far from it, truthfully. We live in tumultuous times, and our daily lives are affected by the enemy, inherent sin, and this sinful world that belongs to Satan. As a result, sometimes even believers get off track. That's why Paul has gone to great lengths to explain and confirm our earthly struggle with sin in Romans 7. He knew all about life's struggles. I've already told you, "All believers will struggle with sin in this life, even Paul." Therefore, we must change our thinking. We must recall the words of Jesus, "...but be of good cheer, I have overcome the world" (John 16:33). He who is faithful has promised. Now reckon it so. The bottom line concerning sin is this. Only Jesus walked this earth and remained sinless. That's why we need Jesus!

As we begin today's lesson, find comfort in these words. "Believers must cling to the rich promises of scripture in the shadow of the cross. There we find mercy, love, forgiveness, and eternal redemption. In this life, even though we may fail, the faithful love of God never fails. As promised, He will see us through!"

Paul assured the church at Philippi that a faithful God would see them through. *"...being confident of this very thing, that He who has begun a good work in you will complete it until the day of Jesus Christ" (Philippians 1:6).*

Day Three: **Receive.** Prayerfully read Romans 7:14-25

1. Although you belong to Jesus and your sins were settled on Calvary, here you are, studying about sin. Romans 7 outlines its work in the lives of believers. You know, "It's finished," but when

you fail or fall into sin, you feel helpless and hopeless. Things look bleak! Nonetheless, based on God's promises, you immediately repent and are quickly restored. Moreover, you believe that God is working all things together for good because you love Him and are called according to His purpose. (See Romans 8:28.) Thankfully, you love God's Word, and you embrace that promise. Free of guilt, you must grab hold of God's promise and endeavor to walk it out. God loves you, and even when we fail, His everlasting love endures. To encourage your faith, prayerfully complete the following verses.

a. **Romans 8:38-39** - For I am persuaded that neither _____ - nor life, nor _____ nor _____ nor powers, nor things _____ nor things to come, nor _____ nor depth, nor any other _____ _____, shall be able to _____ us from the _____ of God which is in Christ Jesus our _____.

b. **Romans 14:8** For if we _____, we live to the Lord; and if we _____, we die to the Lord. Therefore, whether we _____ _____ _____, we are the Lord's.

c. **2 Corinthians 5:6-8** So we are always _____, knowing that while we are at _____ in the _____ we are _____ from the Lord. For we walk by _____, not by _____. We are _____, yes, well _____ rather to be _____ from the _____ and to be _____ with the Lord.

d. Record the perfect promise of John 16:33 below.

2. In Romans 7:14, Paul gives an interesting description of himself as "carnal [or unspiritual], sold as a slave to sin." Closer examination of the verse reveals that Paul is writing in the present tense. He does not write, "*I was* carnal [or unspiritual], rather *I am* carnal...." Through this confession, he is providing believers some critical information. Since Paul wrote and taught about walking in "*newness of life*' and "*dying to the old self*," we can conclude that he had knowledge and authority in this area. In short, Paul knew a carnal Christian when he encountered one. These profound words must have a unique purpose because he has written them under the inspiration and guidance of the Holy Spirit.

What is God telling us through Paul? Thinking biblically, what was the purpose of his profound confession?

3. At the time of Paul's writings, he's a Christian - he's saved and redeemed. Moreover, he's a believer, a church planter, a prolific writer, and a missionary who has faithfully answered God's call. He has abandoned everything to preach Jesus Christ and Him crucified. He has declared emphatically to the Church at Corinth, *"For I determined not to know anything among you except Jesus Christ and Him crucified" (1 Corinthians 2:2).* Paul knew Jesus! His dramatic encounter with Jesus on the road to Damascus left him blinded, yet with eyes to see. God saved him. Paul was a new man - a new creature who walked in newness of life. He had fresh eyes, a new heart, new passion, and purpose. Paul will spend the remaining days of his life writing, preaching, and teaching about Jesus. Until his beheading in Rome, Paul was a faithful bondservant. He was about the Father's business! In Romans 7:14, however, you see what appears to be a contradictory statement. Review the verse. From the original language, Paul confesses that in his "present redeemed state," he is still a creature of both the flesh and spirit. He shares his plight or dilemma in Romans 7:15. Review Romans 7:15 and complete the last phrase below.

"For what I am doing, I do not understand. For what I will to do, that I do not practice;

4. Do the words of Romans 7:15 describe you? If so, you are invited to share.

5. Although Paul has outlined his inner struggle with sin in Romans 7:14-25, he is not alone. Paul's struggle is also our struggle. Read each passage to **identify the struggle** and record your answer below. Be specific. When appropriate, use the words of the verse to answer.

a. What was Paul's inner conflict, and how had it happened v. 14

b. What was in him? v, 18

c. What type of man? v. 24

d. Where was he trapped? v. 24

6. As believers, we hate sin. Furthermore, we hate the struggle with sin in this life. Review Romans 7:15, 19, and 21 to discover the tension of a believer who desires to obey God's law and hates his or her sin. Using your words, *highlight* the main point(s) the following passages.

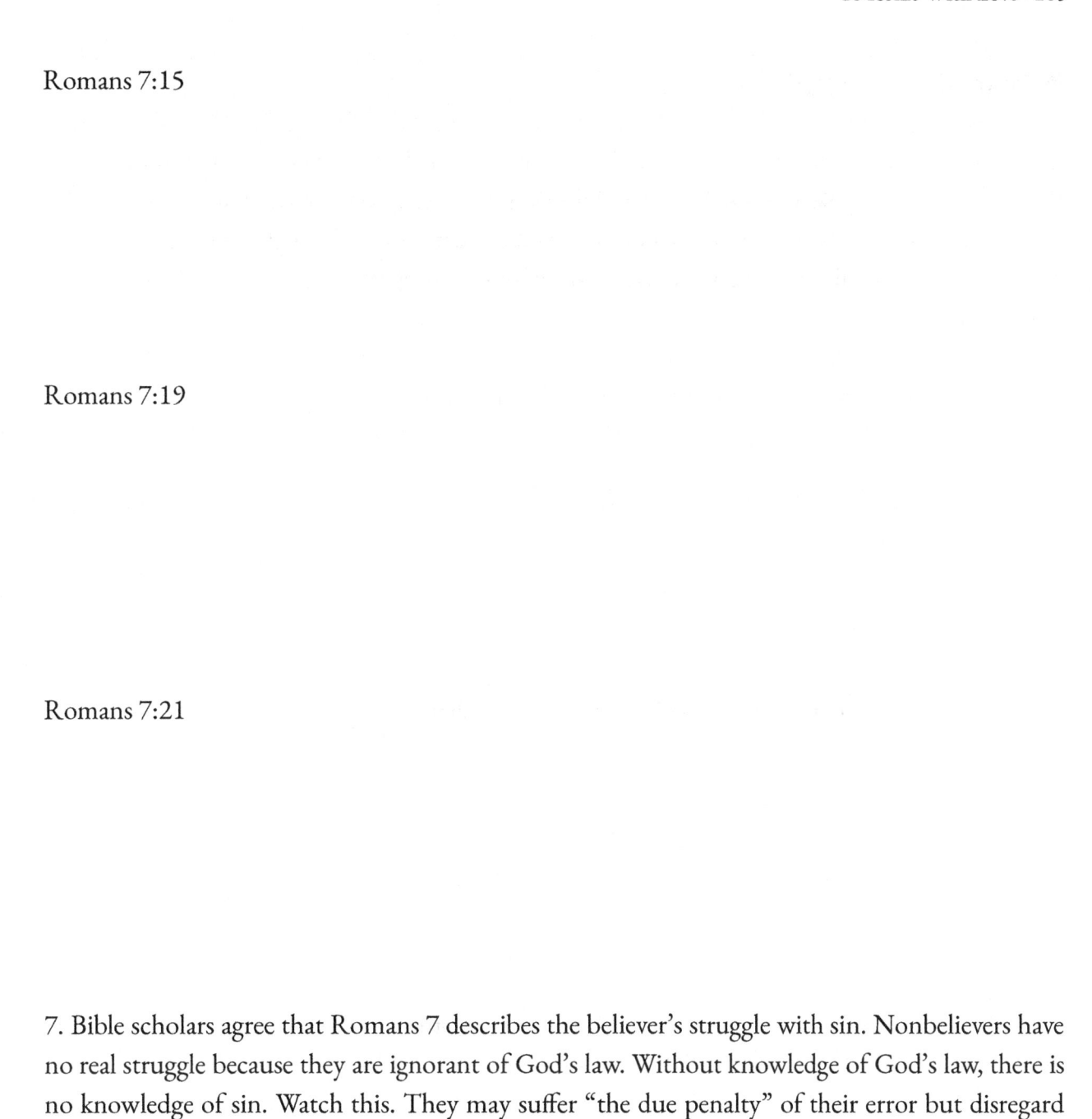

Romans 7:15

Romans 7:19

Romans 7:21

7. Bible scholars agree that Romans 7 describes the believer's struggle with sin. Nonbelievers have no real struggle because they are ignorant of God's law. Without knowledge of God's law, there is no knowledge of sin. Watch this. They may suffer "the due penalty" of their error but disregard God altogether. Read and record Proverbs 9:10 below.

♥ Heart-Check For Today.

8. In Romans 7, Paul was describing not only himself but all believers. Even the most spiritual and mature believers struggle with sin. Sometimes the sin is not visibly seen or acted upon, yet lust and hate occupy their hearts and minds. Be honest; if you evaluate yourself in light of God's righteous standards, you will fall short. We all do. As we begin to look deeper into the lamentations of Paul, consider your own.

    a. Do you have a struggle presently? You are invited to share.

    b. What do you plan to do about it? You are invited to share.

9. The Bible is full of rich promises. Record below the scriptural promise that gives you the most comfort when you fall short, as we all do, even Paul.

Lesson 10: The Struggle With Sin
Romans 7:14 – 25

Day Four: **Reflect.** Romans 7:14-25

Memory Verse: "O wretched man that I am! Who will deliver me from this body of death?

I thank God—through Jesus Christ our Lord!" (Romans 7:24-25).

Romans Road Map. Romans 7 addresses sin in the life of believers. We are all spirit and flesh. At any given moment, we either walk in the spirit - pursuing righteousness - or walk in the flesh, fulfilling deeds that resist God, exposing the ungodly part of man. So far, our Romans journey has brought us to the following conclusions:

1. Sin impacts us all;

"...for all have sinned and fall short of the glory of God,..." (Romans 3:23).

2. God's law reveals sin;

"...I would have not known sin except through the law" (Romans 7:7).

The Revelation of Sin Is God's Gift.

The revelation of sin is a gift from God by the power of His Spirit. Apart from this revelation - there is no repentance - and no path which leads to salvation. As you already know, salvation is the greatest gift you could ever receive. The revelation of sin displays the goodness of God at work in people. He desires that no man perish. (Prayerfully read and review 2 Peter 3:9.) Because of His long-suffering, forbearance, and kindness, those He has chosen and called will come to faith. Long before you were ever born, God knew you, chose you, and called you with divine purpose. Before the foundation of the world, God knew the exact moment you would collide with the revelation of your sin in light of the holiness of God and His standards. He knew precisely when and under what conditions His spirit would be born in your heart and woo you to respond. The Most-High God, the Great I AM, knew you! Rejoice! God always had a plan to save you!

Having the revelation of sin and simultaneously coming to faith is referred to as a "rebirth." It's also referred to as being "born again" or being "born of God's Spirit." These terms describe a spiritual transaction or deposit of God's Spirit in you at the time of salvation. When it comes down to it, all believers are fundamentally the same. We all have the same Spirit of God living in us, sealing and protecting God's Word in our hearts, and bringing it to performance in our lives.

The Struggle With Sin

Although believers possess the same Holy Spirit, Bible scholars believe there are three types of people inhabiting the earth. They include 1). All nonbelievers, and 2). Two kinds of Christians - *carnal* and *spiritual*. From the named categories, it should be easy to understand what that means. *Carnal* Christians are worldly or fleshly. By definition, although saved, they are living after their physical or bodily desires, including all lustful, sensual, erotic, and licentious or lewd acts. They are pursuing and fulfilling deeds that satisfy their flesh. The carnal Christian serves self! Please note, a true believer cannot remain in this state forever because God will prevail. Eventually, the backslider will be renewed and strengthened in their faith and walk. They will return to their first love. The hounds of heaven will not let them go; the battle and pursuit for their soul are much too significant. God will not be denied!

In contrast, the exact opposite is true of the *spiritual Christian*. Their pleasures, pursuits, and desires have eternity in view. In short, their goal is to please God, honor God, and yield their whole being to Him. They seek His will and guidance and enjoy the unity of mind, body, spirit, and soul — their "inner and outer man" – please God. The spiritual Christian serves God, not self.

Conservative Bible scholars believe that at any given time, we're a mixture of both. John Owen has stated the following in *Overcoming Sin and Temptation*. "All Christians have some area of their lives where they live carnally. We are being perfected, but we're not perfect yet." The work of sanctification is ongoing but is not yet complete. Even Paul, a man no one would accuse of being a carnal Christian, confessed in Romans 7:14, "I am carnal..."

This discussion leads us to the topic of today's lesson, which is coming to grips with our struggle with sin. Pastor, teacher, and author John MacArthur stated the following concerning Romans 7:14-25. *"It is a poignant description of someone in conflict with himself, who loves God's moral law, someone who deep down in his innermost self wants to obey God's moral law, <u>but is pulled and pushed away from its fulfillment by sin - sin that is in him.</u> [Emphasis added.]* It is the personal experience of a soul in conflict. It is a battle. It is warfare that rages in the heart... Of that, there is no mistake."

Believer beware! You have been forewarned. The battle between spirit and flesh is genuine and very intense.

1. Review the above paragraph. Notice from Dr. MacArthur's words, referencing believers, including Paul, it's *"sin that is in him."* That's the prevailing issue. Find the emphasized phrase "but is pulled and pushed away...." and underline the sentence. Now reread it. It is the same with us. It's not your husband's sin or your children's, your sister's, brother's, or neighbors' sin. The issue is your sin! Dr. MacArthur's quote identifies the tension of sin and evil within all of us, including you. That's why we are a mixture of carnality and spirituality. New Testament writers agree. Let's review what John and James have said concerning our battle with sin. Read 1 John 1:8 and James 4:17. Record James 4:17 below.

James 4:17

2. God thought a lot about sin. Consequently, a plan was born within the Trinity to overcome it. From a position of radical love, He allowed His only Son to die on the cross to conquer it - SIN - once and for all. Since sin mattered so much to God the Father, God the Son, and God the Holy Spirit, it most assuredly should matter to us. For believers, the issue with sin goes deeper than just admitting that we are sinful and have sinful desires. Prevailing sin, unrepentant sin, and the failure to acknowledge sin is a major problem. The whole world is deceived; everything is out of order. As believers, we must begin to live as part of the solution and not part of the problem. Sadly, as Christians, we have become somewhat desensitized to sin. We don't call it what it is in light of God's holy word. In some cases, shamefully and willfully, we align ourselves with sinful positions not to rock the boat and remain politically correct. Ladies, sin is still sin. God's opinion and position regarding sin have not ever changed. Sin kills and destroys and leads to death - always! **Sin is an**

enemy of God! Because sin is so important, and to expand this line of thinking, we must include failure to call sin what it is - sin. Read and record the highlights of the following verses.

1 John 1:9

Romans 6:23

James 4:4

In 1 John 1:5-10, John speaks frankly about sin. He tells it like it is! In these verses, John addresses false teachers who confessed faith in Christ but denied the reality or evidence of sin.

Additionally, John identifies true fellowship with Christ, and among believers, as other than a "churchy-type gathering." He is referencing a spiritual community with his brothers and sisters in Christ. They were his "fellow" partners, partakers, and recipients in the salvation of God, possessing eternal life. We are in fellowship with "whomever, wherever" they have called upon the name of the Lord. (See Romans 10:12-13.)

3. Prayerfully read 1 John 1:5-10 and complete the following.

"This is the message which we have heard from _____ and declare to you, that God is _____ and in Him is no _____ at all. v. 6 If we say that we have _____ with Him, and _____ in _____, we _____ and do not _____ the _____. v. 7 But if we walk in the _____ as He is in the _____, we have _____ with one another, and the _____ of Jesus Christ His Son _____ us from all _____" (1 John 1:5-10).

v. 8 "If we say that we have no _____, we _____ ourselves, and the _____ is not in us. v. 9 If we _____ our _____, He is _____ and just to forgive us _____ _____ and to _____ us from all _____. v.10 If we say that we have not _____, we make Him a _____, and _____ _____ is not in us."

Thinking on Romans 7, review 1 John 1:5-10 and answer the questions below.

4.

   a. What does it mean to walk in darkness?

   b. Our fellowship with God is jeopardized when we lie and fail to practice the truth. How does this occur? v. 6

c. How are we to walk and what happens as a result?

How?

The results?

d. What happens when we say we have no sin?

e. When we don't practice the truth, what happens? v. 8. Be specific.

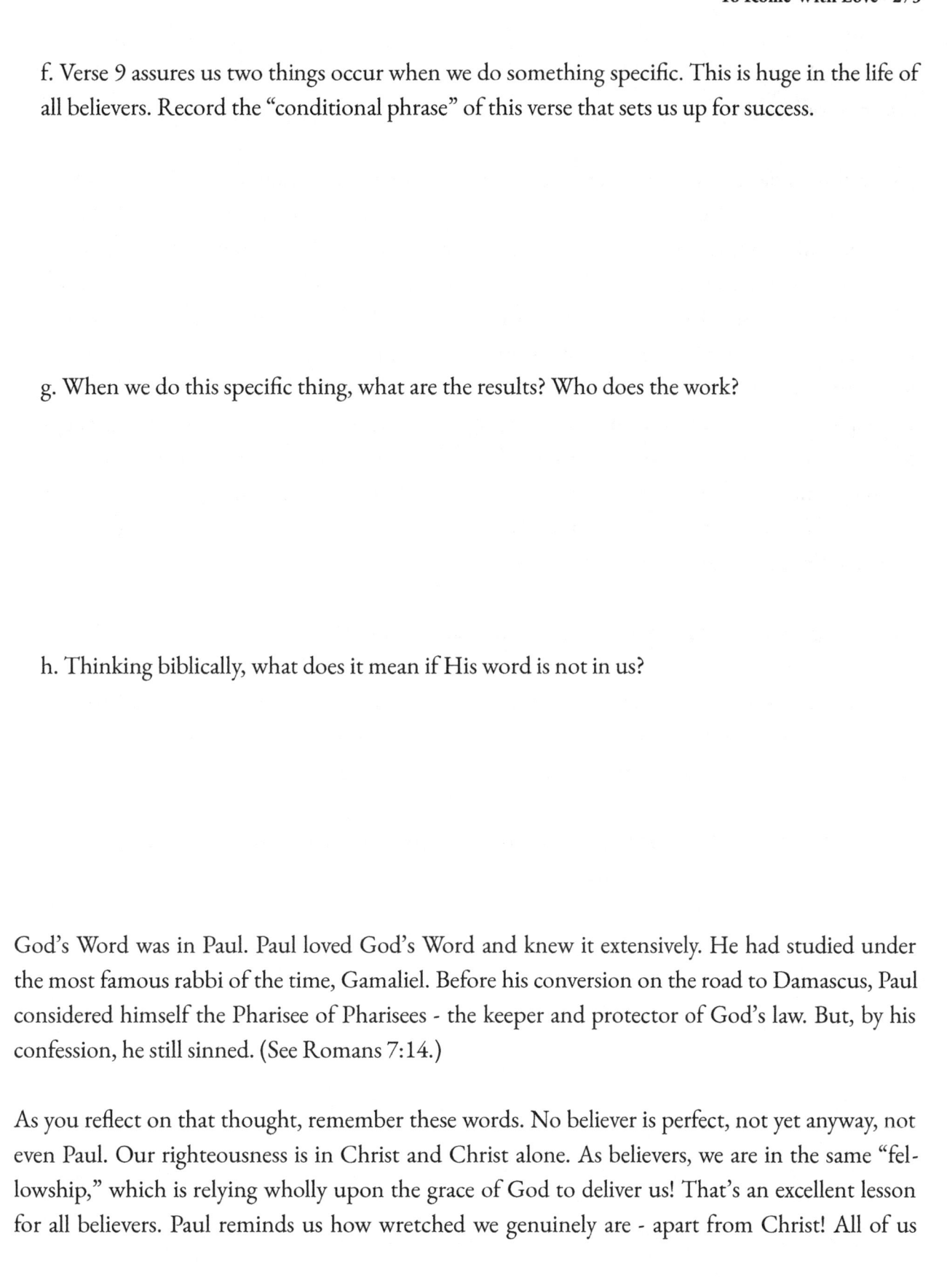

f. Verse 9 assures us two things occur when we do something specific. This is huge in the life of all believers. Record the "conditional phrase" of this verse that sets us up for success.

g. When we do this specific thing, what are the results? Who does the work?

h. Thinking biblically, what does it mean if His word is not in us?

God's Word was in Paul. Paul loved God's Word and knew it extensively. He had studied under the most famous rabbi of the time, Gamaliel. Before his conversion on the road to Damascus, Paul considered himself the Pharisee of Pharisees - the keeper and protector of God's law. But, by his confession, he still sinned. (See Romans 7:14.)

As you reflect on that thought, remember these words. No believer is perfect, not yet anyway, not even Paul. Our righteousness is in Christ and Christ alone. As believers, we are in the same "fellowship," which is relying wholly upon the grace of God to deliver us! That's an excellent lesson for all believers. Paul reminds us how wretched we genuinely are - apart from Christ! All of us have sinned and will sin again. When we do, God will redeem us! He knew we would always fall just short of His glory.

As we close today's lesson, pray for a deeper measure of sanctification in your life and a healthy dose of humility to accompany it. Lest we get puffed up and self-righteous in our thinking that we've got this or we've arrived. As we begin to think we've got this, we start to look upon others narrowly and with a critical eye and spirit. Thoughts like, "I would never make that mistake." or "She must not be saved, surely no believer would do that." or "How can a true follower of Christ say or do such a thing?" or finally, "That would never happen to me." We are in error when we esteem ourselves better or more spiritual than others. Only God knows the heart of man, and the same spirit inhabits each of us. It is easy to see how self-righteousness can lead to the harsh judgment of others - and that, too, is a sin! Why not pull the plank out of your eye before you go there. Then cry out for mercy just like Paul. (See Romans 7:24.) We are all guilty as guilty can be. But, because of Jesus, we are cleansed and forgiven. In essence, Paul is saying to believers everywhere, "Look, if I'm carnal, you need not think you're exempt."

All God's people need His amazing grace. Paul assures us only Jesus can deliver us from these bodies of flesh. (See Romans 7:25.) There is always victory in Jesus! His mercy and grace are not in short supply. We are equally in need of His divine mercy and grace to see us through! Ladies, look up your redemption draws near. Jesus has overcome the world, and He has victory planned for you. You are invited to close in prayer, beginning with Paul's words.

"O wretched man that I am! Who will deliver me from this body of death? I thank God—through Jesus Christ our Lord" (Romans 7:25).

Lesson 10: The Struggle With Sin
Romans 7:14 – 25

Day Five: **Respond.** Prayerfully review Romans 7:14-25

Memory Verse: "O wretched man that I am! Who will deliver me from this body of death?

I thank God—through Jesus Christ our Lord!" (Romans 7:24-25).

Paul's inspired words in Romans 7 have certainly given us a lot to consider. He has pulled back the curtain to reveal the complexity of man's heart (and mind) concerning the struggle with sin. In essence, many thoughts and desires occupy the hearts and minds of believers simultaneously. You may feel overburdened with conflicting thoughts today. Perhaps you're struggling with unconfessed sin. If so, it will wear you down, steal your joy, and render you ineffective to God's purposes, as it always does. Remember, even Abraham had no witness or testimony in Egypt before Pharaoh. God may have used him mightily in Egypt, but even Abraham proved useless when he was caught a in the lie.

That's why sanctification is so important. As women of faith, we need to harness our "good thoughts and desires" for God's purposes and His glory. Too, we must learn to discern, cultivate, and desire Godly wisdom and counsel – from His Word and others. Then, we must respond accordingly. Not out of obligation, weakness, or fear, mind you - but in strength with joy and liberty, which is available to believers through Jesus. You must embrace the challenges before you by faith and not dwell on the what if's or the could've, would've, or should've(s). The fine details belong to God. He has not forgotten you, your circumstances, or where you are spiritually and naturally. His eye is always upon you! Praise Him and trust Him. That's your part. You must leave the fine details to God and then be satisfied with whatever He has planned.

Remember, everything that touches your life has passed through His nail-pierced hands. God loves you, right here, right now, and just as you are! So if you're struggling today, talk to Him – pray first – always. Prayer should be our first response instead of our last resort. So before you begin this lesson, ask Him to search your heart and confess all things before Him. Then, remember this. Everything has a purpose, and nothing that He has planned concerning you will be lost or unredeemed. God will use it all because He intends to use you.

As you wrap up Romans 7, confess that God loves you! Say it aloud – shout it, if need be. Then, believe by faith that God, who loves you, is presently working all things together for good because you're called according to His purpose. Paul said it like this. "And we know that all things work together for good to those who love God, to those who are the called according to *His* purpose" (Romans 8:28).

Beloved friends, God has a plan for you! He is working out all matters concerning you! Trust Him and ask Him to encourage your faith and strengthen your walk as you respond to His Word. Pause now and pray.

1. Using a dictionary, bible dictionary, or concordance define *sanctification*.

2. As you begin to study sanctification, write a few sentences explaining what it means in your life.

You may be challenged as you begin to understand sanctification and its significance in your life. Remember, God is never in a hurry. He is committed to you for the long haul. He is after the authentic, permanent reshaping of your hearts, not merely lip service. Understanding things like the Holy Spirit's work in sanctification and its purpose concerning you will be discussed as you continue on the Roman's journey. That process begins today! In short, sanctification changes you from the inside out, starting with the heart. It makes you more like Jesus. As His only purveyors of truth and love on the earth, this is a must for all believers. You must yield to God's spirit and trust Him through His holy sanctifying work. It may be painful at times, no one dies quickly, and death to "self" is no exception. Sanctification invites you to free-fall with your Savior by His grace and for the benefit of the gospel. Remember, consistently yielding to God takes practice, but it's doable!

Paul was addressing learned men when he wrote to the church at Rome. The men of Rome were ancient thinkers and intellectuals of their time. Surrounded by Roman culture and philosophers, with many Stoics among them, they were champions of debate and dialogue. These mental giants erroneously believed that mere knowledge of God's Word was enough to transform their lives to obedience. However, in Romans 7, Paul declares that mere knowledge of the law is never enough. Paul possessed more head knowledge than the lot of them, and he confessed that it was not enough - even for him. Paul admitted he was still carnal. (Review Romans 7:14.) He knew that knowledge, apart from God's spirit, can never produce righteousness. Instead, it leads to a "heady" legalism and self-righteous works.

3. Are you being guided by your head or your heart? Are you yielding to the Holy Spirit? You are invited to share a recent testimony of your yielding to the Holy Spirit.

4. Obedience to God yields blessings. How has your obedience been rewarded?

5. Paul needed deliverance from his *"body of death."* He was a wise man. You need this as well - we all do. Paul was eager for the transformation that sanctification produces. Have you invited the Holy Spirit to increase or expand this work in your life? God will never force you along. He patiently desires that all believers hunger and long for righteousness, including you.

Are you longing for the transformation that sanctification produces? That will require embracing His presence and yielding to His Word. That doesn't mean picking and choosing which verses you'll yield to and which ones you won't. You can't cherry-pick God's Word! Sanctification requires accountability and obedience to what you know about what God's Word instructs. After all, that's to what you will be held accountable – **what you know from His Word.** Are you willing to practice His presence and yield to His spirit? Yes ___ or no ___ ? If not, why?

6. Most seasoned believers think they have a handle on the significant areas of sin in their lives. That would be things like adultery and murder, but a close examination of the Sermon on the Mount in Matthew 5 - 7 still brings all believers up short. According to Jesus, if you hate someone, you have murdered them, and if you've lusted after someone, you've committed adultery in your heart. You need Jesus and the sanctifying work of His Spirit to make you more like Him. As you grow and mature, over time, your struggle with sin should decrease. Although you may have a handle on the big sins, what about the annoying little sins? Those sins that ooze into your life that you think you've risen above or moved beyond? Your thoughts and motives are suspect, as well. You must be aware lest they trip you up because sin always begets more sin. Examine the list below to discover the little sins that, if left unchecked, can grow into big sins which overtake your life. The list comes from Romans 1:28-32. Do any of these sins sneak into your life repeatedly? If so, put a check in the space provided.

_____cheating – to act dishonorably or unfairly to gain a personal advantage

_____stealing – taking for yourself what God has not given to you

_____covetousness - desiring what God has not given you but has given to someone else

_____judging - forming an opinion or conclusion about someone which is always rooted in pride; to arrogantly esteem yourself better or greater than others _____lying - not telling the truth; anything short of the whole truth

_____strife - conflict, anger or bitter disagreements; "stirring the pot"

_____envy - a feeling of discontented or resentful longing aroused by someone else's possessions

_____gossip – casual or constrained conversation or reports about other people that are generally negative with the intent to hurt, harm or damage their standing. It includes being a party to it in any fashion. but is not limited to spreading rumors or engaging in conversations where others are spreading them

If you've been honest, now you know how to pray. Take a little time to pray about these sinful areas in your life. Remember, God loves you, and He is faithful to hear from heaven and answer your prayers!

7. We are all guilty, even Paul. This author would confess that she has been guilty of all of the above at one time or another. Awareness is the key. Ask God to reveal any particular area of danger in your life. He is pleased to grow your faith and bring His word to performance in your life. A prayer like this He always answers: "Lord Jesus, make me more like you!" King David was faithful to confess and ask for guidance. He was a man after God's heart. Prayerfully read and complete Psalm 139:23-24 below.

"_____ me, O God, and _____my heart; _____ _____, and know my _____; and see if there is _____ _____ _____ in me, And lead me in the way _____" (Psalm 139:23-24).

8. Paul knew what King David knew. Review Romans 7:24-25. Record Paul's 6-word heartfelt cry of Romans 7:24 below.

9. Nonetheless, there will be sin in this life. To exalt and praise God, joyfully record Paul's conclusion from the first sentence of Romans 7:25 below.

10. Sisters, be of good cheer! There is victory in Jesus. You will conclude this week's lesson drawing near to God, and practicing His presence through the prayer of King David from Psalm 103:10-12.

"He has not _____ with _____ according to our _____,

Nor _____ us according to our _____. For as the _____ are high above the earth, So great is His _____ toward those who _____ Him; As far as the _____ is from the _____, So far has He _____ _____ _____ from us" (Psalm 103:10-12).

Words from Jesus
"These things I have spoken to you, that in Me you may have peace. In the world you will have tribulation; but be of good cheer, I have overcome the world" (John 16:33).

Notes

About the Author

Anne is a missionary and a graduate of Metro Atlanta Seminary. She is President of Open Heavens Publishing and its companion nonprofit, which exists for the express purpose of providing biblical curriculum to women in prisons, rehabs, assisted living facilities, and rural churches where economic or physical hardships are demonstrated. Overall, Anne is committed to getting God's Word into the hands of those who are hungry to study but lack provision or resources. Since 2004, she and her husband have remained faithful to their overall mission. Teaching scripture and growing others in faith and practice through the study of God's Word.

Other ministry highlights include outreach to the impoverished, establishing Bible studies in government-funded communities and homeless shelters, facilitating Laundry Love, launching feeding ministries, church planting, and urban city ministry complete with curbside prayer, preaching, and teaching. She and her husband have lived and ministered in four southern states, Mexico and Jerusalem, Israel.

Her more traditional work has included writing, developing, and teaching Bible college curriculum, bible studies, and women's retreats. She has served as a women's leader and facilitated countless small groups at home and abroad, as well as trained and mentored women who will serve as wives to tomorrow's pastors and missionaries, should the Lord tarry. Lastly, she has spearheaded prayer ministry and served as a community pastor in mid-town Atlanta.

Anne's life testifies that God's Word transforms hearts, and she desires to share the word with other women. Her love and passion for God's Word and literal approach to scripture, sprinkled with a bit of humor and frankness about the troubling times and circumstances in which we live, is not only challenging and inspiring but clever and refreshing as well. In short, her inspirational teaching encourages women's faith. She's passionate about women trusting in Christ alone as they come to a fuller understanding of God's Word. Through in-depth Bible study, she motivates them to embrace God's Word - wholly - and challenges them to love it, live it, and trust it!

To date, except for her study, *To Rome With Love*, all of Anne's studies and course curriculum feature biblical truths and insights from women of scripture. She has used the rich texts of their lives to shape and develop every lesson - every story. Her straightforward approach to the facts of scripture and her strong faith and hope in God is mixed with heartwarming, true-life missionary takes and adventures, as well as antidotes and confessions from one woman's heart to another. Anne loves all the women of the Bible and hopes you will too! (A complete list of books and studies is available on her website: annenicholsonauthor.com).

After 14 years of full-time missionary service, she and her husband returned to Auburn, Alabama.

Their initial call to Auburn in 2004 launched a vibrant college ministry on the university's campus.

To date, former students passionately serve in ministry endeavors worldwide. Anne and Jimmy have a blended family of grown children sprinkled throughout the southeast. They include five sons, one daughter, a daughter-in-law, and three energetic grandchildren - two boys and one girl.

You are invited to contact Anne for information about teaching materials, future publications, or to solicit her for a speaking engagement, conference, or retreat at womenofthebible01@gmail.com.